Cornered Poets

Cornered Poets

A book of Dramatic Dialogues

by

Laurence Housman

Jonathan Cape
Thirty Bedford Square, London

First published in 1929

DEDICATION
TO
FRIEND ROGER CLARK,
WHOSE CORNER IN POETS
THIS
COMES TO JOIN

Contents

List of Illustrations

ACKNOWLEDGMENTS *are due to the Directors of the National Portrait Gallery and the Musées Royaux des Beaux Arts de Belgique, to the Trustees of the Carlyle House Memorial, and to the Dean and Chapter of St. Paul's Cathedral, for providing the necessary material in copyright photographs from which the illustrations of this book have been made.*

Introduction

THE particular corners in which these poets find
themselves are not those, at Westminster and
elsewhere, provided by a grateful posterity.
They are only contemporary corners for which
they have mainly to thank fools, and themselves.
Some of the situations here presented had an
important bearing on the poets' lives and characters ; others passed, and were probably forgotten.
Two of them, perhaps, never happened ; the rest
did. But in no case — it need hardly be said — did
the situation resolve itself in the actual form given
to it in these dialogues. This is no work of history ;
only a commentary based fancifully on fact — a
suggestion of the way that poetic natures react
when up against situations not of their own
choosing.

It may be objected that two of my characters
are not poets in the accepted sense. But Carlyle
could never have written his history of the French
Revolution as he did, had he not been more of a
poet than an historian. And Ninon de Lanclos
could not have lived her wonderful professional

life so beautifully and well, had she not also brought to it the poetic temperament. Her corner here comes next to John Donne's ; and to most readers she will surely seem the more pleasing of the two — doing so much better, with her lack of religion, than he with the indigestible weight of it that carried him to his grave.

In the course of these dialogues I have put verse (and occasionally prose) purporting to be theirs into the mouths of my poets : sometimes it is really theirs, sometimes it is not. I leave any reader, who is sufficiently interested, to discover for himself which passages are real and authentic, which are genuine variants of the finally received form, and which are mere imitations fitted in to the body of the text, where required, for lack of the more genuine article.

As regards 'the Cutty Stool,' it is quite hopeless for an English writer who deals with the sacred character of Burns to invite goodwill from his Scottish readers. He will not get it. I have only to say here that the spelling used in that dialogue is a necessary compromise in order to keep it intelligible for the majority of my readers: English with a suggestion of the Scots accent, which those who know the true sound-value can complete to taste.

L. H.

The Fire-lighters

Characters

THOMAS CARLYLE.

JANE WELSH CARLYLE.

JOHN STUART MILL.

MRS. TAYLOR.

THOMAS CARLYLE
By Samuel Laurence (Carlyle's House Memorial Trust)

The Fire-lighters

A DIALOGUE ON A BURNING TOPIC.

March 6th, 1835.

The low, square parlour, with its staid furniture and small-patterned paper, is occupied by two people of homely appearance, seated to right and left of the fireplace, who, though silent and self-engrossed, have yet an air of companionship. For here are two wise heads that have come together to make the best they can out of characters which most people would find impossible to live with, and which they find difficult. Mrs. Carlyle sits with a book in her lap, which she reads across her knitting. Carlyle has books at hand, but they are not open. Smoking a pipe that has almost burnt out, he sits looking into the fire. His wife glances across at him, but does not stop her knitting — hardly her reading — as she asks :

MRS. CARLYLE. More coffee, Carlyle ?

*(A delayed shake of the head is all the answer
she gets.*

*Sounds in the passage outside attract her
attention : in a not very pleased voice,
she says :)*

Here he is ; and somebody with him.

*(And the door opens to admit (in the maid's
queer way of announcement : " Mrs.
Taylor, ma'am ; and Mr. Mill, sir ")
first a lady of striking appearance, very
consciously graceful in all her movements,
and behind her a smallish man, not
nearly so middle-aged as he appears,
intellectually handsome – distinguished
even, if one could see him alone ; but
his present accompaniment with her pale
vivid personality, has almost the effect
of effacing him : indeed, he seems to be
very anxiously effacing himself, and it
is more as a worm than a man that he
quivers into the room. The lady, however, flowing spaciously toward their
now risen hostess, leaves him exposed to
the greeting of Thomas Carlyle, whose
hand he takes and presses tremulously,
and, in a voice sharp with distress,
begins to throw himself on the other's
mercy.)*

14

MILL. Oh, my dear Carlyle, are you never going to speak to me again ?

CARLYLE. Why, we'd almost gi'en up expecting ye ; but ye've come. And what, Ma'am, has brought you out so late the night ? This is an honour to which we're not accustomed.

MILL. Yes, yes. Oh, I'm sorry if we are late. Did I definitely name a time ? You had my letter ?

CARLYLE. Saying you'd be looking in after supper. Supper with us has been over an hour and more.

MILL. Oh ? Has it ? I'm sorry ! Oh, but something so terrible has happened. How to tell you – almost impossible !

(*He hovers, manifestly distraught, while Mrs. Taylor, with her assuaging presence, benignantly presides over him.*)

MRS. CARLYLE. (*Whom perturbation always annoys.*) Won't you sit down ?

(*Mrs. Taylor does so with the air of conferring a benefit on the chair which she selects : Mr. Mill still hesitates.*)

MILL. Oh, I hardly know how to sit down, with the news I have still to break to you !

MRS. TAYLOR. (*Fervently calm.*) You had better sit down, Stuart; you will be less agitated. Mr. Carlyle, Mr. Mill has something terribly painful to tell you.

MILL. Yes, indeed, most painful! The most untoward thing that I have ever known to happen. If you were not my friend, if I were not so sure of your great strength of mind and character——

CARLYLE. Is it a death, you mean, that you are telling me?

MILL. One might almost say " yes " – of a loss so complete, so irretrievable. But though not a death in the technical sense – oh, such a terrible fatality! And it was only yesterday, at ten o'clock yesterday morning, that I discovered it. I'm sure I don't know how to tell you about it.

CARLYLE. Not to be told is, maybe, more painful, Stuart Mill, while one is waiting.

MILL. Yes, yes; but how to begin without first fully explaining!

CARLYLE. How to explain without first beginning, ye'll find harder, I'm thinking.

MRS. TAYLOR. (*Cutting the agony short with surgical skill.*) It is about a book of yours, Mr. Carlyle – a manuscript.

MILL. (*Grateful for the assistance.*) Yes – oh, thank you! Now I can tell you! Carlyle: that French Revolution manuscript which you lent me to read – the first volume – and which I had put away so carefully, to wait till I had more time for it: an unfortunate, a most unfortunate thing has happened! My dear Carlyle, nearly the whole of it has gone – disappeared utterly!

> (*The news has a different effect on its two recipients: Mrs. Carlyle, stiffening into rigid hostility, sits erect; her knitting has stopped. Carlyle crouching forward, looks up in stricken bewilderment to ask:*)

CARLYLE. Gone? Has it been taken?

MRS. TAYLOR. (*Concisely handling the Gordian knot.*) Destroyed.

MILL. (*With a grateful gesture to his goddess for her assistance.*) Yes, destroyed.

CARLYLE. What, do you mean, has destroyed it?

MRS. TAYLOR. Burnt.

MILL. Yes, burnt. Oh, most unfortunate!

CARLYLE. (*Dazed.*) Burnt? My manuscript burnt? How? Where?

MILL. In a fire.

CARLYLE. (*Trying to see the sense of it.*) Burnt, in a fire ? In your own house, you mean, you've had a fire ?

MILL. Alas, no ! *Lighting* a fire ; lighting a great many fires. I fear. My maid did it.

CARLYLE. (*In funereal stupefaction.*) Lighting fires ! Your maid lighted her fire with my French Revolution ?

MILL. With the manuscript, yes : almost the whole of it. Oh, if I had but known sooner !

CARLYLE. (*Puzzling it out.*) Ye mean, if ye had known sooner, ye'd have stopped her doing it ?

MILL. I might then, at least, have saved most of it. But that such destruction should have taken place under my own roof is too terrible for words !

(*Carlyle takes up a piece of paper, and starts making a spill of it.*)

CARLYLE. Aye, words ; what's the good of words—ever ? It's well to be thinking that, with so many that I've wasted time on—gone now, you tell me, to their last reckoning. . . . Gone to light a fire ; there's a sort of sense in it—somewhere, that, maybe, I shall see presently. Words, words, just words !

(*He takes up his pipe, and stoops to light the spill.*)

MRS. TAYLOR. It was, as Mr. Mill will be able to explain, Mr. Carlyle, one of those unforeseeable accidents which do sometimes occur ; and when they do, so doubly distressing to everyone. Mr. Mill—you see how terribly he is still upset by it— has suffered over it beyond words. He tells me that last night he had not a moment's sleep.

(*The spill has burned itself out ; the pipe stays unlighted.*)

MILL. Not one moment, I assure you. Oh, I couldn't !

CARLYLE (*Meditative.*) Burned. Was it for having read it that she burned it ?

MILL. (*Too agitated to take in the philosophy of this inquiry.*) No, no, no ! She had no idea !— most unfortunate—hadn't any idea *what* she was burning. It was there, with other papers, waste-papers, put to go away. That also I shall have to explain. Oh, I do so want you to understand how it all came about—one thing upon another—such a concatenation of circumstances ; so that she actually did it not knowing—nobody knowing.

CARLYLE. (*After a weighty pause.*) And—*when* was it done ?

MILL. " When " I can't exactly say. It was not done all at once. Oh, if I had known, if I had dreamed of such a possibility! But, as I say, I only discovered it yesterday!

MRS. TAYLOR. And then, immediately, he came to consult *me* about it ; so difficult to decide how best to break it to you. I advised him to write first, making an appointment, and then come and explain personally.

CARLYLE. But why didn't you come at once, man ? Why waste time, putting it off ?

MILL. Oh, I was too distressed — too distressed really to know what to do about it.

MRS. TAYLOR. It also took some time to find out exactly *how* it happened. And there was still just the possibility of finding fragments thrown away that had not been burned. It seemed better to wait — in case. But even the waiting — and nothing more found — was terrible!

(*And now Mrs. Carlyle speaks ; and it would be out of character if it were not done with devastating intent.*)

MRS. CARLYLE. Coffee, Mrs. Taylor ?

MRS. TAYLOR. Thank you, no! Coffee at night kills me, Mrs. Carlyle.

mrs. carlyle. (*Meaningly.*) Then I can't persuade you ?

mrs. taylor. Thanks, no, really !

> (*Defrauded of one death, Mrs. Carlyle turns
> hopefully to effect another.*)

mrs. carlyle. Coffee, Mr. Mill ?

mill. (*Welcoming the diversion.*) Oh, thank you ;
I really don't know whether I ought to. It's too
kind of you to offer it. Well, just half a cup, then.

mrs. carlyle. Sugar ?

> (*But this would be too much, he feels :
> pleadingly he declines.*)

mill. *No* sugar.

mrs. carlyle. (*As she hands it.*) I'm afraid it's
not as hot as it was an hour and a half ago.

mill. (*Feeling it with his spoon.*) Oh, but it is
still warm — quite sufficiently warm, I assure you.
So kind of you, I'm sure !

> (*And while he sips the cup of her deceptive hos-
> pitality, Carlyle with a sigh resumes
> speaking.*)

carlyle. Aye ! ye meant well, I don't doubt.
But ye'll forgive me that I haven't got my

thoughts clear about it yet. All burned, ye say ? Twenty-four hours have given ye the advantage — you knowing how it happened.

MILL. How it happened ? Ah, yes ; that, at least, I can explain quite fully. Not to suggest, — no, not for a moment — that it relieves anyone — me least of all, of a terrible responsibility. But you will, at all events, understand better, when I have explained.

CARLYLE. Aye ; when a thing's been done, it's better for one to know how it *has* been done, than how it hasn't been done — if circumstances have left ye the choice.

MILL. Oh, it isn't a question of choice, I assure you ; I wish to conceal nothing : but the whole situation is so difficult !

MRS. TAYLOR. (*Soothingly.*) Mr. Carlyle will quite understand, Stuart, when you *have* explained to him.

MILL. Oh, yes ; the explanation is not difficult. But how to find a remedy is what now troubles, and distresses, and so pre-occupies my mind. My dear Carlyle, I put the manuscript away, as I have said, for an occasion of more leisure. I put it away, perfectly safely, as I believed, but — not knowing — upon a heap of old manuscripts to which my maid had been in the practice of helping herself for fire-lighting purposes. *She* had put them there — *I* had not — in a corner next to the fire-place in my study, so as to be handy. And your manuscripts being on the top of these — I had put it there, thinking it would be such a nice dry corner for it, other corners being sometimes damp. — Well, your manuscript being there, on the top, she began helping herself to it, every day when she lighted the fire — and I not knowing ! There you have the situation. Think of it ! My own fire, Carlyle, by which I worked, lighted every day with pages from your precious manuscript. And to think that I have sat by that fire and warmed myself at it. Oh dear ! how could she have done it ? How could she have done it ?

MRS. CARLYLE. (*Knifing him with her common sense.*) Very easily, apparently. She had matches.

MILL. Oh, yes ; but a manuscript, and such a manuscript !

MRS. CARLYLE. (*Acidly.*) I suppose, in your house, she is accustomed to seeing a lot of waste paper lying about.

MILL. That is so, of course. I am constantly sorting out old papers and manuscripts to go away and be burned.

MRS. CARLYLE. Then that accounts for it. Oh, I daresay she didn't notice the hand-writing, and thought it was yours.

MILL. No ; she can't read. Oh dear ! Oh dear ! Had she been able to, it might not have happened.

CARLYLE. How long, do ye reckon, has she been lighting the fire with it ?

MILL. How long ? Let me see ! I was away ill ; I came back a month ago. And it was certainly all there then ; I have a recollection of seeing it. You gave me the manuscript, you will remember, in January ; I was away till the beginning of February. Two days later I had a fire in my study, and resumed work ; so that would be just over four weeks ago.

CARLYLE. Five hundred sheets in thirty days : seventeen a day or thereabouts. She's not sparing of paper over her fire-lighting, I'm thinking.

MILL. I'm afraid not ; she's Irish. But I have, Carlyle, one small bit of consolation for you, — oh, that it had been more !

(*He has dived into his pocket ; and now produces the bit of consolation for a peace-offering.*)

The last fifty pages were still left ; I was in time to save them — forty-seven, to be exact.

CARLYLE. (*As he turns them over.*) Aye, there's mercy to be found even in small numbers. There's three weeks' work saved to me at any rate. And how did you find your Irishwoman out — what she was doing ?

MILL. Untidily she had left some of it lying on the hearth ; and suddenly I saw your hand-writing on a piece of paper. Never, never so long as I live, shall I forget the horror of that moment — as I realised what had been done. Oh, believe me, Carlyle, how far rather I would have had this happen — as it so very easily might have happened — to one of my own writings. Every time I think of it my distress becomes greater.

MRS. TAYLOR. I am quite sure Mr. Carlyle believes you, Stuart. You must not distress yourself more than he does.

MRS. CARLYLE. And with us waiting to hear what the more important Irishwoman had to say about it.

CARLYLE. Aye ; go on, man — if there's anything more you want me to know.

MILL. I rang the bell. The other servant came. I said, " Send Bridget to me." I waited for her, a long time ; at last she came ; she said she had been tidying herself : she didn't look like it ; but then —

being Irish—she never does. I showed her the piece of burnt paper : I asked her where she had got it—though, of course, I had looked already, so knew. And when she had explained, then I told her what she had done.

MRS. CARLYLE. Did it distress her, Mr. Mill ? —unnecessarily, I mean ?

MILL. No : I'm afraid not. She said she had taken the paper from where she had always taken it—from the top of the last bundle I had given her to be burned. And that explained it. Without saying a word to me about it, she had put it there —in the shelf by the fire-place—so as to have it handy in the mornings. And I—not knowing : that is where I had placed your manuscript.

MRS. CARLYLE. (*Ambiguously*.) And you considered that a good defence ? What did you do to her ?

MILL. Oh, nothing ! What could one do ? It was no use dismissing her for a pure accident. I told her she had destroyed a work of far greater value than all the other contents of the house put together—a statement which I could see she had not the competence to believe ; and I told her never, never to do such a thing again.

MRS. CARLYLE. Unless the " thing " was given

her for the purpose, you mean ? And what did she say ?

MILL. (*Obsessed with explanation.*) Well—as I say——

MRS. CARLYLE. (*Snubbingly.*) I asked you what *she* said.

MILL. Oh, she proposed praying to some saint or other—St. Anthony, I think she said—to get it back for us. And then, beginning to cry—seeing how very much upset I was—she asked if she was going to be blamed for it. Well, what could I say ?

MRS. CARLYLE. Yes, what could you ? What did you, Mr. Mill ?

MILL. I—oh, I said it wasn't a question of *blaming* anybody ; just one of those impossible, unpredictable things which none could have foreseen. Of course, in a way, she should have told me that she had put her fire-lighting papers there ; but then—*why* should she have told me ? you will say. And yet, *that*—her putting them there and *not* telling me—that is how it all happened ! Oh, most unfortunate ! If one were so foolish as to believe in what is called " intervention " surely this alone would be sufficient to prove the contrary ! What but blind destiny can account for a tragedy so fantastically, so monstrously unreasonable ?

27

MRS. CARLYLE. Any more coffee, Mr. Mill ?

MILL. No, no, thank you ; no more. Oh, that such a catastrophe should have wiped out the work of your great mind !—and before I had even had the chance to read it : for then—then my memory of it might have helped you.

CARLYLE. Why trouble, man ; why trouble ? In fifty years from now nobody would be reading it. It's gone out sooner ; that's all.

MILL. I cannot so console myself. Who knows yet how important your work is not going to prove ? No, it is a terrible tragedy. I don't know anything—I never have known anything happen like it. And so little that I can do ! Still, of that — if you will allow me—I did want to say just a word.

(*Nervous and deprecating, he looks at Car-lyle, whose heavy ruminative silence does not encourage him. So once more his angel comes to the rescue.*)

MRS. TAYLOR. Mr. Mill wishes to say that any expense which the reconstruction of the work will involve—he will be only too happy——

MILL. Oh, it will be a privilege : the one small act of reparation I can make to you. Of course you still have your notes ?

28

CARLYLE. (*Dejectedly*.) Last week I burned them.

MILL. Dear ! dear ! dear ! How most unfortunate !

mrs. CARLYLE. Very careless, wasn't it ?

MILL. Oh, but I make a point always — do, in future, make a point, Carlyle ; I make a point never to burn anything till I have had the printer's proofs of it. You see, one never knows.

mrs. CARLYLE. We shall know better in future, Mr. Mill. The point shall be made.

MILL. But you still have the books I lent you, and the others that I borrowed ? You marked passages — references, did you not ?

CARLYLE. I marked nothing. The books were not mine.

MILL. Oh, I'm sorry ! In future pray do so with anything that I lend you. Treat them as if they were your own.

CARLYLE. Eh, I'll know my way about a book once I've got through with it. And there's much not set down that, happen, I'll still remember – have the idea of, anyway. Put to that — I've the brain-knowledge, somewhere ; it's not all gone out of me.

MILL. Oh, I'm so glad; and I am sure that it will be so. For you have a wonderful memory, Carlyle.

CARLYLE. But there's more bits I shall forget. Eh, better so. There's some things I was for reconsidering; but didn't make the time for it. Now I shall have to. Aye, if I've faith enough to tackle the job, the book'll be the better in the end for it, as the world's better for many things that happen to it that it doesn't like.

MILL. It's very generous of you, Carlyle, to take that view. I wish I could. But no; I have no right to. I still don't feel that I can forgive myself; though not directly to blame—still, the manuscript was in my hands; and here it is you who have to face the consequences.

CARLYLE. It's done, man! What use talking more about it? If't had happened that I was dead, 'twould have been harder for ye to put right then. But I'm still alive; still with some power of body and brain; still with enough health and will for the gae'ing forward. And between them, she and her saints have saved to me forty-seven pages to light my ain fire with for a fresh start. Aye, it'll not be so hard speaking of it when 'tis all done, as maybe it is now. I've knocked down a spider's web, times not meaning it, and seen him start again the next minute; and by morning, there was his web again. I've only to have the determination of a spider in me, and this'll be done too.

MILL. It's good to hear you take it so philosophically, Carlyle. You give me the best kind of comfort that in such a case can be given. And of course, anything that I can do in any way—any advance, I mean, or secretarial assistance that I can provide, to make up for what I fear must be a delay of at least six months in the publication, that you must allow me to insist upon; there I have a right that you must recognise.

CARLYLE. Aye. We shan't quarrel about that.

MILL. Nor, I trust, about anything, now that all has been explained. But if by any chance you should be finding it hard to forgive me for the unconscious share I have had in the disaster: then, Carlyle, I only ask you to imagine the position reversed and consider—would you not rather be in your own now, than in mine? I believe you are generous enough to recognise that mine is the harder one; for you now, having the strength for it, have the remedy in your own hands; while I, for my part, have to depend entirely upon you. To be so helpless—that indeed is terrible! And helpless, except for you, is how I feel myself.

CARLYLE. Helpless ? No man is helpless that can give help to others. You've offered me help, and I'm accepting it. If you hadn't,—hadn't been able,—or hadn't the wish to—helpless you might then call yourself. It's a curious thing, I'm thinking : there's more things I should have altered — left out, or put differently—that I let by at the time—that now are coming back to me. But shall I be able to express them so well as I did first ? One way of getting to know more, is finding that you know less. But that's a depressing thought when ye're going over old ground again. It's like times when I go to Ecclefechan where I was born ; there's more sadness in that now, than there's pleasure, I find. For it isn't the joys, but the faults of youth that come back to ye, then. And though one may know better now, one can't put any of those things right again—not into place as they happened. Your chance for that is all over and gone. But here anyway there's a chance left — for ye can do more with a book than with your back life—though that, too, may have gone to light fires that had better not been. That's just a thought for ye—as it came.

MILL. A very interesting one. Yes, I suppose for most of us it is in our youth that we find, looking back, the things we most regret. But in all my life, Carlyle, I don't think I remember ever having had such an ordeal of misery and distress, and unavailing regret, as I have experienced since I made the terrible discovery which brought me here to-night. Over and over again I review it, re-examine it, question it, turning it this way and that in my mind, and finding it so fantastically unbelievable that at moments I have almost persuaded myself that it cannot be true ; and then once more brought back to the fact that it *is* true, and that I was the unwitting cause of it. It is the recurrent thought that such a thing could not have happened in a sane world, which makes it the most mysteriously unreasonable thing that has ever befallen me since I can remember !

CARLYLE : Aye : but 'tis when things fall to one like that, that a man must either find a reason, or he must put his reason away from it—one or other. For me, if there's any reason to this, I'll face up to it till I find it. For you, if you can find no reason for it—put it out of your mind, man ! If ye've no place for it, let it go ! Already for me it's wearing an old face, like as if I'd known it before it came to be. You're keeping it on a raw place ; it's doing ye no good. Put it away, man ! Don't distress yourself any more. Enough said.

MILL. My dear Carlyle, I'm so grateful ! I don't think anybody could have been more kind

and considerate than you have been. And I can't
go without saying again——

CARLYLE. Oh, don't say it *again*, man!

MILL. No, no, then I will not! But at least—
not without saying, what I haven't said yet—not
sufficiently : how much you have helped me, how
much indebted I am ; how much I must thank
you for your noble forbearance, and generosity,
and your great self-restraint under—under very
trying circumstances. Believe me, Carlyle, I have
never felt for you so much respect, admiration—
even reverence, I would say—as I have to-night.

CARLYLE. Nay ; we're all but small things, the
best of us, and where's our strength, if we don't
hold together the best we can ?

MRS. TAYLOR. I think, Stuart, we had both
better be going home now.

MILL. Yes, yes. Everything I had to say I have
said, I think. It has been—painful, of course ; but
now, a great relief.

> (*There is a general rising. Mrs. Taylor
> makes the first move. Mrs. Carlyle has
> gone promptly to the bell.*)

MRS. TAYLOR. Good-night, Mrs. Carlyle.

MRS. CARLYLE. Good-night.

34

CARLYLE. (*Forestalling further expressions of gratitude.*) Good-night, man ; good-night.

MRS. CARLYLE. Good-night, Mr. Mill. I hope that to-night you will manage to sleep better.

MILL. Oh, I shall, I am sure. I make no doubt of it.

CARLYLE. I'll see ye to the door.

MRS. CARLYLE. (*Correctively.*) I've rung, Mr. Carlyle. Don't go down and start talking it all over again at the door. You'll catch cold.

MILL. No, no ; don't think of it ! Not for a moment ! Good-night.

> (*And so, with a little manœuvring for position, and the door being domestically opened to emit them, making Carlyle's attempt superfluous, they are gone.*)

> (*As Carlyle walks back to his place, his wife hears the groaning sigh which the presence of his visitors has restrained. Laying down her work she looks up as he passes her chair, and for the first time her voice has kindness in it.*)

MRS. CARLYLE. Aren't you going to kiss me, Tom ?

CARLYLE. (*As he does so.*) That's kind of ye!

MRS. CARLYLE. My dear, it isn't *kind*! It's a " thank God ! " for getting rid of them! What use to us could they be ? This is for you and me, and no one else in the world : you and me *together*.

> (*Carlyle has shifted to the mantelpiece, where he stands looking down into the fire ; but she still holds his hand for a moment or two.*)

He at his bleatings, and I—shut up in a box with no lid to it—not able to give you word or sign how my heart was breaking for you—couldn't come near you ! Oh, my dear, my dear !

CARLYLE. You think I didn't know that, without any flag-wagging to tell me ?

MRS. CARLYLE. There are some things a body starves if it can't say. We weren't given our senses and affections never to show them.

CARLYLE. (*As he goes to his chair.*) Aye ; but *there's* always the danger.

MRS. CARLYLE. There isn't any—now *they've* gone !

CARLYLE. Aye, gone ! Mercy has come to us at last !

MRS. CARLYLE. And quite time it did, to save

36

the wits of one of us ! Here have we been sitting like a pair of pin-cushions for him to jab words into ! Words, words ! Saying the same thing over and over again—no beginning and no end to it !

CARLYLE. Aye ; a sore visitation this—to both of us. What's it to prove ?

MRS. CARLYLE. That you can be great over it.

CARLYLE. Oh, if only I had the faith for it ! Would God that I had the faith ! . . . But I haven't.

MRS. CARLYLE. I'll have the faith for it, if you'll have the courage, Carlyle. Aye, you are hurt and sore wounded ; but you've been a hero.

CARLYLE. What have I done, woman, to be called a hero ?

MRS. CARLYLE. That you didn't kill him ! And you didn't skin him, either !

CARLYLE. No need ; you did that for me.

MRS. CARLYLE. (*Vengefully.*) If he'd as many skins as a cat has lives, I'd have liked to have all of them ! What did he sit there for, talking, talking ? Why—when he'd given you the plain facts of it couldn't he go ?

CARLYLE. He wanted sympathy.

37

MRS. CARLYLE. And you gave it him! My dear, you were wonderful; but it nearly killed me. There was I crying my inside eyes out, tender as a lamb-cutlet—for *you*, my dear; and—for *him?* wanting to jump up and scream " You blind fool, for God's sake, get out ! " It almost pulled me to pieces, that did ! Carlyle, don't harden yourself now, there's no need for it. I'm not wanting sympathy, I'm wanting the man's blood !

CARLYLE. Aye, like ye would ! But what for, if you had it ?

MRS. CARLYLE. Just to know that he *hadn't* it. Bleed a man, and he's harmless—comparatively— for the time being, at any rate ! But oh, my dear, my dear ! all your work—those months while I've watched and waited, and you've grunted and grumbled at yourself, and said you'd put the whole thing into the fire, if you could have your wish, and begin again ! And now it's come—happened ; and you see what a dear fool you were— and always will be ; for you'll never alter. All your life you are going to be miserable, grinding out things the world will remember you by, and doing it like a dog scratching out fleas all the time ! And I've got to kennel with you while you are doing it ! Don't harden yourself to *me*, Tom ! Talk to me ! I said I didn't want sympathy ; it's

38

a lie ! I do ; I need comforting. If you don't comfort me, I shall go out and murder the first man or woman I meet — as a substitute for the one that's escaped me.

CARLYLE. D'you want that poor girl's blood too, she that did it ?

MRS. CARLYLE. She ? That girl ? I don't believe a word of it ! 'Twas that woman, with her six feet of virtue reaching to the skies !

CARLYLE. Tut, tut ! Ye're mad on that woman.

MRS. CARLYLE. She's mad on herself. That's what's wrong with her : a self-worshipping goddess, she is ! So much worship he's poured over her, she's caught it from him ! Did you see her sitting there — lapping up the situation, and enjoying it — thinking how dramatic it all was ! — like a crocodile drinking milk ! How do we know that she didn't give the Irishwoman the papers herself ?

CARLYLE. Aye ; when ye've no facts — the next best thing is to shape them to your ain liking.

MRS. CARLYLE. One fact's plain enough anyway ! She's jealous of you for daring to be a greater writer than that tame cat of hers. And don't forget, Mr. Carlyle, he'd started on the same thing himself, and gave it up when he heard you were

39

doing it : which did show he'd some sense at any rate.

CARLYLE. Aye ; and was kind over it, too. Handed me on his books and materials. Ye mustn't forget that.

MRS. CARLYLE. *She* didn't think it kind of him. She's had it against you ever since. And it's my belief, Carlyle, that if she *knew* of his having your manuscript (which of course she did) she'd never rest until she got hold of it. And then who knows *what* she wouldn't do ?

CARLYLE. Ye'd better sit down and write a play of it. Eh ! women are strange creatures, and fine fighters — left to themselves ! If they hadn't men to tame them, 'twould be a bloody world, I'm thinking. So she did it, eh ?

MRS. CARLYLE. She saw that it *was* done, I'll be bound ! There's a girl that can't read ; and fires always being lighted ; and what he writes goes into them — *after* it's been printed — "Always make a point — do in future make a point of *that*, Mr. Carlyle ! " — And what's easier for that woman than to make an altar of his rubbish, and put you for a victim on the top of it ?

CARLYLE. Aye, Jane, my lass, — now you are enjoying yourself ! Go on !

MRS. CARLYLE. I enjoy finding the truth about people, and telling it. Show me the outside of a thing, and I'll tell you its character, if its got any. It wasn't for your outside, Tom, that I took *you*. And though your inside's not so attractive either, I've never repented. It's never struck me to say that we are happy together ; but if anything were to put us apart, I'd scream down Heaven with curses on those that did it. Now ; do you believe me ?

(He sits inscrutable : and she continues.)

What's happened now was to *me* as much as to you, every bit. I've got to have six months' worse growlings because of it : and maybe, all the time, not a word of kindness shall I get from you. And I'll not ask it; it's the price I pay for having you. So, if you wouldn't mind, Mr. Carlyle, just for once — before you begin beating me again — if you wouldn't mind letting me have the assurance — from something you say now, or do — that the beatings I get do *you* good anyway ! I'm not going to flatter you by pretending that they do *me* any ! It only just happens that to-night I want a word of comfort and reassurance, from the only being who can give it to me — that I am not useless, though I may no longer be ornamental.

(Having said her say, and conscious that she

41

*has said it rather well, she sits experi-
mentally expectant, satisfied that, anyhow, something has got to come of it.
After enjoying the somewhat prolonged
silence that ensues, she says :)*

I'm waiting, Mr. Carlyle.

CARLYLE. Maybe if I gave it you, it 'ud spoil
you.

MRS. CARLYLE. We'll risk it.

CARLYLE. I don't like risks : I've got the Scot in
me.

MRS. CARLYLE. Then you don't like me : for I'm
the biggest risk you ever took in your life.

CARLYLE. (*Admiringly.*) Eh, that's true ! The
woman has got me.

MRS. CARLYLE. Have I ? I'm not so sure of it.
Have you got *me ?*

CARLYLE. If I hadn't. . . . Yes : ye can take
this to your comfort, if it is any comfort to ye !
. . . If I hadn't *you*——

(*So far he gets but no further ; and after
giving his pause its measure, she speaks
again.*)

MRS. CARLYLE. It's hard to get out, isn't it ? —

42

that without me would make any difference big
enough to find a word for. Never mind : try!
You needn't say it in terms of affection. Just
state the fact.

CARLYLE : Aye : there ye go! I could have
sworn to it. Always shall I have ye interrupting
me just when I've a thing to say that, maybe, was
worth saying ! Eh, where have I put my pipe ?

MRS. CARLYLE. It's in your own hand.

(*He proceeds slowly to fill it, but does not
light it.*)

CARLYLE. What was I to tell you ? You want
me to exaggerate ? I'll not. Put it this way, and
let that content ye—That if I hadn't you, here,
always troubling me, that burnt sacrifice would
never get itself written again. But it's going to be.

MRS. CARLYLE. Yes ; and a work for two of us—
don't make a mistake about that ! It's not going
to make me happy, Mr. Carlyle ; six months of
growlings and complaints never did that for a
woman. But it's going to make me proud of you.

CARLYLE. Aye : a proud day for both of us—
this, first and last !

MRS. CARLYLE. That we ever let those two go
out alive ? I'm not so Christian.

43

CARLYLE. No: but ye've that in you that makes up for it. . . . (*Then as he slowly rises.*) So, now I'm going to my bed.

MRS. CARLYLE. To begin your reading ?

CARLYLE. Yes, to begin my reading, where it's never left off, and never will. . . . Good-night to ye, lass.

MRS. CARLYLE. Good-night, Tom.

> (*He moves to the door, then comes back and lays a hand on her.*)

CARLYLE. Eh ; if it's understanding you want, I was the right man for you.

> (*Having said that he goes. She stands looking after him till the door shuts : then, according to economic habit, turns to poke out the fire for the night. While she is doing so, the door again opens, and a head comes in.*)

CARLYLE. Ye'll see I'm called the right time to-morrow – early ?

MRS. CARLYLE. I'll see you called, Tom, the right time every day, till the Day of Judgment.

CARLYLE. She was late one day — so there now !

(And this time he really has gone. With a jerk of the head and a confirmatory poke at the tumbling cinders Mrs. Carlyle's face takes on its normal expression once more. " Carlyle's himself again ! " it seems to say. The expression is not exactly a happy one, but there's humour in it : she is conscious that Thomas Carlyle is her man, and that no one else in the world would get within miles of managing him as she does.)

The Messengers

Characters.

WILLIAM BLAKE.

WILLIAM HAYLEY.

CATHERINE BLAKE.

ELIZABETH BLAKE.

TWO SOLDIERS.

WILLIAM BLAKE
From a painting by Thomas Phillips, R.A. (National Portrait Gallery)

The Messengers

*At the window of a low cottage-chamber, looking out
into a thatched porchway, the door to which stands
open, sits William Blake busy at engraving. Still
in the early forties, his face beginning to look aged,
but his bodily vigour undiminished, you see him in
the very height of his powers — those powers which
are so troublesome to friends who, in the worldly
sense, wish him well. It is one of these friends
who, after a tap at the door, now enters, and brings
the industrious worker briskly to his feet. From
the far corner of the room another has also risen :
Mrs. Blake, laying aside her work, drops a
humble curtsey — the curtsey expected of inferior
rank by a superior. Blake's bow, on the other
hand, is much more nearly the nod of an equal.
Greeted by name, Mr. Hayley enters, and without
waiting for invitation takes a seat. Handsome,
stoutish, elderly, well, almost elegantly, dressed, he
carries himself with an air of importance — his*

D   49

face, the face of a man who is pleased with him-
self ; and the foolish kindness of that false esti-
mate is conferred also on others. A vain, amiable,
but not very trustworthy character, he adores the
power of patronage which easy circumstances
enable him to exercise. During the last year or
two Blake, conveyed especially for that purpose
from London to Felpham, has been its almost daily
recipient ; and during the process each has become
more conscious of an operation about which they
take somewhat contrary views. Mr. Hayley has
now come charged with something more than
usually definite to say ; and without preliminaries
he broaches what is presently to become a com-
plaint :)

HAYLEY. I have been in the library, looking at
the fresco portraits, Mr. Blake.

BLAKE. I am sorry you have, sir ; you should not
have done so with my consent till they were
finished.

HAYLEY. (*Correctively.*) My own library, Mr.
Blake.

BLAKE. Why, yes, sir, when I have it ready for
you. But when you have a guest and offer him a
bed, you don't get into it *with* him, do you, sir ?

HAYLEY. A commission, Mr. Blake, is different
from a bed — don't you think ?

BLAKE. I do, sir, indeed ! It is far more important. If you disturb my sleep by getting into my bed, that is nothing ; but if you disturb my inspiration by looking at my work before it is done, it is the inspiration of eternity that suffers.

HAYLEY. Yes, yes, Mr. Blake ; but if one does not look at the work until it *is* done, it cannot be altered — not so easily.

BLAKE. I do not intend altering it, Mr. Hayley. My visions come to me too clearly for that to be possible. I do not begin to paint a vision till I see it. When I have seen it the vision does not admit of alteration.

HAYLEY. But these are *portraits*, Mr. Blake, or are supposed to be ; and I do not find them very like their originals. A portrait should be a portrait.

BLAKE. If a spiritual form can be called a portrait. My paintings are the spiritual forms of men whom you have not had the advantage of seeing, as I have.

HAYLEY. Seeing ? Ah, yes : with you believing *is* seeing, is it not, Mr. Blake ?

BLAKE. Can any man see without believing ?

HAYLEY. Perhaps not ; it is only a question of which comes first — the sight, or the belief in it,

BLAKE. Surely the belief, sir ! Why, if I did not believe, I should see nothing, through not knowing what to see.

HAYLEY. But I saw you, Mr. Blake, before I had any *degree* of belief in you. I saw you before I knew who you were.

BLAKE. Then you did not see me, sir ; but only my spectre.

HAYLEY. Spectres vanish : you didn't.

BLAKE. I should have vanished if your mind had not exercised itself, and caused me to remain and become real to you.

HAYLEY. Pray explain yourself.

BLAKE. Why, sir, was it not in the light of day that we first met ? You believed it was day ; had you not believed it was day, you could not have seen anything. You saw something coming toward you : you believed it to be a man. I was that man. Had you not believed me to be a man, could you have discovered anything about me that was true ?

HAYLEY. Why, no : put it that way, Mr. Blake, of course not. But—had I met you in the dark, and believed you to be a woman ?

BLAKE. Why then, sir, you would have perceived that part of me which *is* woman, but which ordinarily my male spectre causes to remain invisible. We are every one of us both male and female, Mr. Hayley, in the sight of eternity.

HAYLEY. Dear, dear ! Mr. Blake ; don't say such things ! Someone might hear you. Medical science, my dear sir — medical science refutes any such——

BLAKE. Medical science refutes everything it knows nothing about. Science is the Devil's way for trying to put truth out of countenance and to substitute falsehood. A man who depends on science is a fool.

HAYLEY. But Newton, my dear sir, Newton — the subject of one of your pictures — Newton was a great scientist.

BLAKE. Newton would have had no science had he depended on it. All that he discovered was by imagination. But, in order to convince blockheads, he had to put it mathematically — otherwise they would not have believed him. Newton never talks mathematics to me : he knows better. If he did, I should paint him with his face to the wall.

HAYLEY. Really, Mr. Blake, you surprise me ! With his face to the wall ? That would be a very curious portrait : the back of a man's head—most original !

BLAKE. Sometimes the back of a man's head tells more than his face—is the most truthful thing about him. Only yesterday Voltaire came and asked that he might sit to me.

HAYLEY. Voltaire ? But Voltaire is dead, my dear sir !

BLAKE. The vegetable Voltaire is dead, sir ; but his spectre—the most powerful part of him—is as much alive as ever it was. I found him sitting in the closet, sir.

HAYLEY. My dear Mr. Blake, how very awkward !

BLAKE. Not at all, sir. I got him out without any difficulty. He wanted to sit to me, I refused to do him such honour. "Your face," I said, "does not please me." At that he made a characteristically ribald remark, and presented me with a different part of his person. Then I perceived on the back of his head a large wart. That decided me ; and I did his portrait—if you like to call it so—on the spot. It is there on the closet wall, if you care to go and look at it. And if you would like to have that in your library——

HAYLEY. No, no ; I think not. Warts are not

pleasant. Though, to be sure, Cromwell had warts, had he not ? But Voltaire, I never heard that Voltaire——

BLAKE. Voltaire's wart was a spiritual one, and only shows in the world of the imagination. When I saw it, it had the complete face of Rousseau upon it ; so if I give you the back of Voltaire's head, you will have Rousseau's face to admire as well. That is what makes it so truthful a portrait ; for the two are emanations from the same spectre.

HAYLEY. Mr. Blake, if I did not know you so well—hearing you say such things, I should think you a very—well, a very strange person.

BLAKE. I am a strange person, sir, to anybody who believes in his own spectre more than he believes in God.

HAYLEY. In his own spectre, Mr. Blake ? I never imagined that anybody was supposed to have a spectre until he was dead.

BLAKE. Why, it is then, sir, that he has his best chance of escaping from it. When he is dead either he gets rid of it, or it carries him down bodily into Hell, where—being the more powerful part of him—it causes him to remain, a delusion of the senses to all eternity.

HAYLEY. What a terrible fate !

BLAKE. It is a fate which many people undergo, even in this life, sir, with the firm conviction that they are enjoying it. And if you try to persuade them otherwise, they think you " a very strange person."

HAYLEY. But how do you *know* these things, Mr. Blake ?

BLAKE. I know them as all the poets and prophets of eternity know when the word of the Lord comes to them.

HAYLEY. And what do you mean by " the word of the Lord," Mr. Blake ?

BLAKE. All the images of eternity which the life of the senses seeks to obliterate.

HAYLEY. But the word of the *Lord*, you say. How, even if you hear, can you be sure of it ?

BLAKE. I can be much more sure of it than I can be of a man's word, which I hear plainly with my outward ear. *That* I have often had reason to doubt ; but when the word of the Lord comes to one, doubt is impossible. Are you not sure when you feel indignation—when you experience pity, or love ? What makes a man more sure than courage that he has not to fear death ? Or is he who, with his whole heart, forgives an injury ever guilty of wrongdoing ?

56

HAYLEY. No, Mr. Blake : in that sense, what you say is very true. But when you spoke of the prophets——

BLAKE. I spoke then as the prophets spoke, having the same ground for my conviction—no more and no less. Isaiah was able to declare the word of the Lord because the word of the Lord was in him ; and for no other reason. And Christ was able to declare himself divine because the divinity of God was in him. And you and I are divine for the same reason : that we appear less so is because of the life of the senses which separates us from Him.

HAYLEY. My dear Blake, I believe you to be a sincerely religious man ; but I fear your religion would rather frighten—rather shock most people.

BLAKE. It is better to have a religion that shocks people than one that only sends them to sleep. And where, pray, do you find more people asleep of a morning than in church during sermon time ?

HAYLEY. Very true ; but then, I so seldom go——

BLAKE. And if you did, you would sleep like the rest of them, and I shouldn't blame you. And yet they dare to call *that*—" preaching the word of the Lord." When the word of the Lord comes to

57

me, it doesn't send me to sleep ; it wakes me, aye—
even at the dead of the night. Doesn't it, Mrs.
Blake ?

MRS. BLAKE. It wakes both of us, Mr. Blake :
and it's little sleep we get afterwards, for the rest
of *that* night. Oh, it so excites him, Mr. Hayley,
there's no keeping him in bed ! Up he gets and
has to write it all down. And then I generally get
up too, and make him a hot posset or a cup of tea.

HAYLEY. Well, that must be a very interesting
experience. But don't you think there is something to be said for putting everything in its place
—the right thing at the right time—so that you
have a time for everything in turn ? In that way
there is much to be said for church-going, when
people, having nothing else to do, can collect
their thoughts and direct them in—well, in the
proper direction.

BLAKE. That is the Devil's favourite arrangement. You could not have stated it better.

HAYLEY. Mr. Blake, you surprise me ! I'm sure
the Devil does not favour church-going.

BLAKE. Why, he goes himself, and is the most
regular in his attendance ! Generally, when *I've*
been to church, it was the Devil who did all the
preaching and the praying.

HAYLEY. Really, my dear Mr. Blake, the things you do say ! Perhaps you'll think some day that *I'm* the Devil !

BLAKE. No, dear sir and friend, I don't think you are the Devil, for you always mean well. But I think the Devil has sometimes come here in your form to tempt me.

HAYLEY. Here ?

BLAKE. Yes, here, sir ; and not long ago either.

HAYLEY. Pray, when ?

BLAKE. When was it, Mrs. Blake, that we received a visit which we began by supposing was from our kind friend here — and then as he went, seeing his hind view, I said " There goes the Devil ! " ?

MRS. BLAKE. The last time you said that, Mr. Blake, was three o'clock last Wednesday.

HAYLEY. (*Much scandalised.*) But I came to see you *myself* last Wednesday.

BLAKE. Of course, the Devil would have you to think so, Mr. Hayley, wishing to have you on his side, and to cause bad blood between us. But don't let him deceive you again ; he didn't deceive *me*. The moment I shut my vegetable eyes, and opened my spiritual, I saw him in his true form.

HAYLEY. (*With a growing stiffness.*) But what — if you will allow me to ask — was he trying to persuade you to do ?

BLAKE. To paint a pair of hand-screens for a lady of title, who wanted them to screen her own paint from the fire ; also to go on with some miniatures that would bring me more money than a design of Adam and Eve in their state of innocence which — on the commission of the Holy Ghost — I was then doing instead.

HAYLEY. (*At last obtusely perceiving.*) But that — that is precisely—— (*He breaks off.*) Mr. Blake, are you intending to insult me ?

BLAKE. Certainly not, Mr. Hayley ; but it would be insulting my own intelligence to accept such advice myself, or to suppose you capable of offering it except the Devil had made you his vehicle.

HAYLEY. (*Rising.*) Mr. Blake, Devil, or no Devil, I am speaking now according to the intelligence which God has given me ; and that, I venture to think, is not inferior to yours. And let me tell you that ever since you came here I have had your interests far more at heart than you have yourself; and I have done everything—everything I could—to introduce you to the best people—people of influence and quality, and people of means; yes, and even of title. To keep you in work here entirely myself—that was not to be looked for, and I did not promise it. But I have noticed—I have noticed with pain and growing concern—a certain parade of independence which you—" put on," shall I say?—yes, put on, when I speak to you about working more profitably; for I do not think you have it at other times. And I might—taking your own line of illustration—say that when you do that it is the Devil who is making use of you. But I know it is not—it is only your unfortunate republican principles; which are also the reason, let me tell you, Mr. Blake, why you do not prosper and get more commissions.

BLAKE. Commissions—commissions, sir? And pray, whose image and superscription have they, do you suppose? What would Jesus Christ say to me if he found me with my hands full of such commissions, and coining money by them instead of making representations of the Divine Image as it has declared itself through the men of genius of all ages? Am I to imperil my eternal salvation for commissions, sir?

HAYLEY. Mr. Blake, let me tell you that you are talking nonsense!

BLAKE. And let me tell you, Mr. Hayley, that what appears nonsense to you is divine truth to me! I have a great respect for you, sir, and for your opinions when you keep them to yourself; but when you try to make them be *my* opinions, and would have me rule my conduct by them, accepting commissions contrary to my conscience, and even to my liberty, then I think the most charitable supposition I can make is that the same thing is happening again to-day which happened last Wednesday!

HAYLEY. Mr. Blake, you are sadly forgetting yourself, and not only yourself, but our respective positions — yours and mine. But I have so high an esteem for you, when you are truly yourself, that I think the kindest thing I can do now is to terminate this interview. And if, as I go, you perceive me carrying a tail, I beg that you will advise me of it, for I do not wish to carry anything off your premises which does not belong to me!

BLAKE. I would not so suspect you for a moment, sir. I am sure you are not capable of carrying away anything from here which is not your own.

> (*After this Mr. Hayley has no more words to waste on his antagonist, but he is nevertheless a person of good manners; and as*

he makes hastily to the door he turns to
give parting recognition to one who has
done nothing amiss.)

HAYLEY. I wish you good morning, Mrs. Blake.

MRS. BLAKE. Good morning, sir.

(*But the offended gentleman has already gone.*
Looking at her adored man with troubled
eyes, she breathes an invocation of his
name, then stops.) Oh, Mr. Blake !
(*But Blake is not heeding her. The light*
of battle still shines in his eyes ; but
there is an amused look on his face.
Fiery he may be : but he has the sweetest
temper in the world.)

BLAKE. The cauliflower puts forth a thorn !
The roasted sheep a threatening horn !

I don't think I have ever liked him better, or found
the man more to my mind ! Damn braces, bless
relaxes ! The thing needed saying, and now it's
been said.

MRS. BLAKE. Oh, but you've hurt his feelings,
Mr. Blake !

BLAKE. Hurt his feelings ? How have I hurt
them ? Have I prevented him from seeing the sun
rise to-morrow : made it harder for him to believe

that a lark sings better than he does, or the roaring of the sea sound less to him ? If in any such way I had prevented his feelings, I should have hurt them. But if I have helped him to know that he's a fool, I have not hurt them—I've done him a service.

MRS. BLAKE. But you haven't, Mr. Blake : you've only made him know that you *think* him a fool.

BLAKE. Well, if he has any respect for my opinion, as he pretends—and it isn't only *my* opinion, woman, I'd have ye know ! . . . I might have told him what Socrates said of him yesterday ; but I didn't !

MRS. BLAKE. What did Socrates say, Mr. Blake ?

BLAKE. He said he was the hind-legs of an ass.

MRS. BLAKE. The hind-legs ? Where was the rest of him ?

BLAKE. In eternity, I imagine, for, he being an eternal ass, there's no beginning and no end to him. Socrates said something about me, too—which I might have told him, for his good.

MRS. BLAKE. What about you, Mr. Blake ?

BLAKE. Why, it was really about me that he said the other thing—else *he'd* never have been mentioned. Socrates told me that I'd tied myself to the hind-legs of an ass — which, by God, is true! For now the ass has spoken, and I know.

MRS. BLAKE. You must feel like Balaam, then.

BLAKE. Yes ; like Balaam, when, consenting to be bribed by a king, he went to tell lies, and call down darkness out of light on the children of Israel — he knowing better all the time ! Woman, have you ever tried to kindle a black flame in the light of noon ?

MRS. BLAKE. No, Mr. Blake, never.

BLAKE. Then don't ! That's what I've been doing here with him : riding on his back all the while, and he paying for it. Now, if I've made him kick me off, I'm glad of it.

MRS. BLAKE. That means we shall go back to London, I suppose ?

BLAKE. We shan't go *back* anywhere. Whether we go to London, or Jerusalem, or Jericho, it's *on*, it isn't *back*. No one has ever gone back to the same place wherever it was, not since the world began. London will never again be the London we knew — that was a portion of time ; we have passed through it — just as we pass through the meals we've eaten, or the clothes we've worn. To go back to them you must roll yourself on a dung-heap—or go rummage at the rag-picker's.

mrs. BLAKE. I don't want to do that, Mr. Blake.

BLAKE. Then don't talk about going back to London ; else you'll be turning yourself to a pillar of salt.

mrs. BLAKE. No, Mr. Blake ; though I shan't be sorry to, for this place has been bad for my rheumatism.

BLAKE. It's your rheumatism that has been bad for the place, my good woman ; just as Mr. Hayley's foolish notions about art have been bad for it. The place is infected : I don't wonder the visions are angry with us : the sooner we get away the better. Here I find myself every day groping in thick darkness, and all the other plagues of Egypt—including the death of Hayley's first-born, for which he expects *me* to go into mourning, four years after the event ! And now he comes to pretend that he knows what Socrates was like better than I do who talk with him every day. Yes, somebody had already told me that he'd been in and said that none of them was like anybody.

mrs. BLAKE. It's very foolish of him, Mr. Blake ; but he doesn't know any better. And I'm sure he's been very kind to us.

BLAKE. He has always been very kind letting us know of it ; and letting everybody else know ! Mr. Hayley has been using me as an occasion for virtue. To-day he has gone away forgiving me, and despising me at the same time.

MRS. BLAKE. But isn't it quite right to forgive people ?

BLAKE. It's a detestable crime, woman, to forgive those whom you have injured. What would you think of me if, after beating you for something you hadn't done, I forgave you on condition you never did it again ?

MRS. BLAKE. I should say you weren't quite yourself, Mr. Blake — only Balaam, or somebody.

BLAKE. (*Impulsively.*) Kate, you are an angel ! (*Then, resuming the argument.*) No, but when Hayley does that sort of thing he *is* himself.

MRS. BLAKE. But how has Mr. Hayley been beating you ?

BLAKE. By exercising the hind-legs of his vanity on an art about which he knows nothing — and then saying — " Well, well, we won't quarrel about it — we'll just leave it ! " Having kicked it to ruins, he ends by showing Christian forgiveness and forbearance about it ! And that man sets up to be my patron : and not mine only — but

67

Homer's, Spencer's, Milton's, Shakespeare's, and all the rest whose heads I am to cut off from Eternity so that he may have them to please his fancy.

MRS. BLAKE. It's very wrong of him, Mr. Blake. But now you get yourself ready, while I go and help Sister Lizzy lay and dish up the dinner.

BLAKE. Sister Lizzy shall do it herself. I've still things I want to say to you. Kate, it's a great mercy that this has happened. I was blind, and now my eyes are opened. Here have I been, for the last three years, making not only myself but others prisoners and captives, chaining them in fetters to the walls of that dungeon he calls his library. Aye, who knows ? Perhaps the fool was right after all ; and I have not seen the true spiritual face of one of them, but only their spectres.

" When Hayley finds out what you cannot do,
    That is the very thing he'll set you to ! "

And here have I been, day after day, dragging them from the realms of eternity to fill odd corners in the place where he goes to enjoy himself, supposing himself to be somebody — as if they could ever be fit company for him ! And *his* portrait to be in the place of honour, if you please ! Yes, that is what makes him so impatient ! That's why he goes poking his nose into the library to see how it's going on. It's his own portrait he's looking for. I've put off doing it to the last, as a man puts off his death ; but it's there — waiting to be done. And the other day, as I sat looking at the space left for it, I saw the ghost of a flea come out and settle on that very spot.

MRS. BLAKE. Good gracious, Mr. Blake ! Has a flea got a ghost ?

BLAKE. A flea is all ghost, woman ! But when released from the flesh — its own flesh, I mean — its appearance becomes much larger, and may, to the eye of imagination, equal the size of a man. This one was the size of Hayley, and was wearing the same clothes — red-brown — and while I was contemplating it, all at once the apparition opened its mouth and stuck out its tongue at me : I drew the outline of it at once — there on the spot ; so if Mr. Hayley came upon *that*, it would account——

> (*At this moment the sound of a voice, drunken and truculent, comes from the garden. Looking out they see two red-coats in a very staggering condition talking across the hedge to the gardener. The voice is loud, and for all its thickness of utterance, the words carry.*)

SOLDIER. So you are working for that bloody

Republican, are you ? Call yourself an English-
man ?

> (*From the inner room, anxious and a little*
> *panic-stricken, comes Sister* LIZZY.
> *This, apparently, is an old trouble.*)

LIZZY. Oh, William, shut the door, bolt it !
It's that drunken soldier again.

BLAKE. What business brings him here, now ?

LIZZY. I'm afraid our poor Thomas has picked
up with him. I've seen them together more than
once. Oh, dear ! now he has come in !

BLAKE. Then now he goes out again. (*He*
advances to the door.)

LIZZY. Take care, William ! There are two of
them.

BLAKE. If they are a hundred, I care not. (*And*
out he goes. The two women stand at the door
anxious, listening to what follows.) Mr. Red-coat,
will you please to take yourself off my premises ?
Aye, both of you !

SOLDIER. Damned if I do ! I'm not here to be
ordered about by a bloody Republican. England's
not for your likes : England's a free country. God
save England !

BLAKE. Amen ! The prayer is needed.

SOLDIER. *Free* England!

BLAKE. Which it never will be, till freed from men like you!

LIZZY. Oh, Kate! Stop him! Stop him!

Mrs. BLAKE. Nothing's going to stop him now, Lizzy. Go and get the dinner.

(*And meanwhile the* SOLDIER *has been having his say.*)

SOLDIER. Who you're saying that to? I'm a soldier of the King. Fight for King and country! Fight *you*, you bloody Republican.

BLAKE. And that you will not, my fine fellow, for I shall not allow it.

SOLDIER. What were you made for but to walk on, you piece of dirt?

BLAKE. No more words! Out you go!

SOLDIER. God save King George!

BLAKE. Aye from you; and all servants of Satan! Go to your Master!

SOLDIER. You say that to a man in his King's uniform.

BLAKE. In any uniform! Damn you, and damn

your King ! He's not *my* King. Your King is the Devil !

(*This scares even Mrs. Blake.*)

MRS. BLAKE. Oh, Mr. Blake !

BLAKE. Now then, off to your own kingdom ! Will you march, or must I make you ?

> (*Apparently he must be made to. He makes a lunge at Blake, staggers, and before he can recover himself, Blake has him by the elbows, and, with incredible energy for so small a man, has run him down to the gate ; and the gate being no longer open, over it he goes. In another moment Blake has reappeared under the porch ; his quarry, the second red-coat, squares up to him.*)

MRS. BLAKE. Oh, Mr. Blake, dear Mr. Blake, don't ! You'll hurt yourself !

BLAKE. Woman, hold your peace ! I'm enjoying myself !

> (*And evidently he is ; the second soldier, showing fight to all points of the compass but one, follows the first over the gate into the road, where together they lie helplessly biting the dust.*)

72

MRS. BLAKE. Oh, well, it's in God's hands now, and He knows best what to do.

> (*They hear* BLAKE's *voice outside, giving directions to the gardener :* " Thomas, see those men don't come in again!" *Then he reappears.*)

BLAKE. Kate, woman, the next time the word of the Lord comes to me, don't interrupt !

MRS. BLAKE. (*Meekly.*) No, Mr. Blake.

BLAKE. It's not a woman's business.

MRS. BLAKE. Why, of course it isn't.

BLAKE. Now remember ! Lizzy, is dinner ready ?

> (*Lizzy scurries off to her household duties, leaving Mrs. Blake to face the prophet alone.*)

MRS. BLAKE. Why, Mr. Blake, your coat's all torn at the shoulders ! Take it off, and I'll mend it.

BLAKE. You shall not. Lizzy shall mend it.

MRS. BLAKE. But she's getting the dinner.

BLAKE. Then let it wait.

MRS. BLAKE. Which ? The coat or the dinner ?

73

(The question receives no answer. For Blake is now getting his reward for letting himself go. "The word of the Lord" comes to him. And while it does so, Mrs. Blake sits down reverently and waits.)

BLAKE. He made me to sow the thistle for wheat, the nettle for a flourishing dainty.

I planted a false oath in the earth; it has brought forth a poison tree.

I have chosen the ape for a councillor, the dog for a schoolmaster to my children.

I have blotted out from light and living the dove and the nightingale.

I have allowed the earthworm to banquet at my door; I have taught the thief a secret path into the house of the just.

I have taught pale artifice to spread his nets upon the morning.

Therefore have my heavens become brass, my earth iron, my moon a clod of clay,

My sun a pestilence burning at noon, a vapour of death in the night.

What is the price of experience? Do men buy it for a song?

Or wisdom for a dance in the street? No, it is bought with the price

Of all that a man hath—his wife, his house, and the visions that are his children.

74

Where art thou, O thought? To what remote land is thy flight?

If thou returnest to the present moment of affliction

Wilt thou bring comforts on thy wings, and dews and honey and balm;

Or poison from the desert wilds, from the eyes of the envious?

Does not the great mouth laugh at a gift? And the narrow eyelids mock at the labour that is above payment?

Does he who contemns poverty, and he who turns with abhorrence from usury

Feel the same passion—or are they moved alike?

Does the whale worship at thy footsteps as the hungry dog?

Or does he scent the mountain prey because his nostrils wide drink in the ocean?

Does his eye discern the flying cloud as the raven's? Or does he measure the expanse like the vulture?

Does the still spider view the cliffs where the eagles hide their young?

Or does the fly rejoice because the harvest is brought in?

Does not the eagle scorn the earth, and despise the treasures beneath?

But the mole knoweth what is there, and the worm shall tell it thee !

(There is a pause. The words of prophecy have ceased : and Mrs. Blake once more thinks of the dinner. "Aye! It's wonderful!" she says, rising ; and is crossing the room to make domestic inquiry, when through the door something catches her eye : she stops and looks out.)

MRS. BLAKE. Oh, Mr. Blake, here is Mr. Hayley again !

BLAKE. *(Without looking round.)* Not again, woman. His toils no longer hold me. This is his angel that is coming. Is there not a light round him ?

(Blake has risen, and now, becoming practical, is taking off his coat.)

MRS. BLAKE. *(Obedient to the vision.)* Yes, I think there is, Mr. Blake. He's coming in a great hurry.

(And in a great hurry, at that moment, Mr. Hayley enters.)

HAYLEY. *(Speaking according to the light which Blake has perceived in him.)* My dear Mr. Blake,

what have you done ? What have you done ?
Word of it is going everywhere !

BLAKE. God's will, sir, to the best of my
ability ; and have torn my coat in the doing of it.
Wife, give that to Lizzy. (*She takes it and goes.*)

HAYLEY. But the King's uniform ! Oh, you
should be more careful ! The King's uniform !

BLAKE. With the Devil inside it—as I told him.

HAYLEY. Yes ; he told me that you said that.
Knowing that I was a Justice of the Peace, he
spoke to me.

BLAKE. Then, sir, you can certify that he was
drunk.

HAYLEY. Yes, yes : drunk, of course. Oh, but
the King's uniform ! And also—what is much
worse—that you not only said *he* was the Devil,
but that the *King* was the Devil !

BLAKE. I said no such thing, sir. I said *his* King
was the Devil, which is true.

HAYLEY. But it was the King's uniform—*our*
King's uniform—he was wearing, Mr. Blake.

BLAKE. Well, it cleared the gate ; *his* coat didn't
get torn. What's *he* complaining about ?

HAYLEY. About your language, Mr. Blake. I'm
afraid—oh, I don't know what will happen !—

most dangerous ! In these days, it's sedition, you know. And now he is going to charge you — summons you. It may even be a warrant : you may be arrested. Of course, I will go bail, I will speak for you ; and I will get others to speak for you — people of influence whom you have met at my house, whose word may count. Oh, but most unfortunate ! — for with things so — our close relations — I share in it !

BLAKE. You are very good, Mr. Hayley ; indeed, you are most kind and generous, after what has occurred between us. And I ask your pardon sincerely, if I have been rude to you, or if I am ever rude to you again. But the people of influence I meet at your house will not be of such use to me as the people of much greater influence I meet at my own. If this case comes before the court, *they* will speak for me, Mr. Hayley, and will convince everybody.

HAYLEY. Dear me ! Mr. Blake, I did not know you had any such friends. Whom, pray, do you mean ?

BLAKE. Moses and the prophets : Homer, Dante, to whom you yourself introduced me — they are both now intimate friends of mine. Raphael will speak for me, Michael Angelo will speak for me. Milton also, though, like you and me, we often differ in our opinions. Will they not hear them, do you think, when I say they are my friends and teachers ?

HAYLEY. (*Still trepidant.*) Yes, yes, I know what you mean, Mr. Blake ; and it is all quite excellent. But they are all of the past—" dead " we call them ; I know you don't agree, but you know what I mean. But to speak for a man's character, in a case like this, you require living people, people of standing and influence.

BLAKE. Oh, if it is someone of influence in our own day that you require, I will call Thomas Paine, of whose *Rights of Man* I have a copy here in my house. He, at least——

HAYLEY. My dear sir, you distress me infinitely —nay, you alarm me ! Thomas Paine ? Never mention him, or you are a hanged man ! As for that copy—hide it, burn it ! Oh, Mr. Blake, what can you be thinking of ?

BLAKE. I am thinking, Mr. Hayley, of the very good service I once did both to him and my country by getting him safely out of it. I got him away to France only just in time ; for if he had stayed, it is very probable that Mr. Pitt—whose myrmidons were already after him—would have made us guilty of his blood. Now, mainly through me and my timely warning, he has become a

79

Frenchman, which most men of your thinking, Mr. Hayley—judges, magistrates, and juries—would surely greatly prefer. His religious views, I know, are abominable; but his *Rights of Man* has never been refuted, and cannot be, for Isaiah, Jeremiah, and Jesus Christ all helped him to write it; and it was, indeed, written from eternity—his being merely the hand which made it visible to our corporeal eyes. *The Rights of Man*, therefore, forms a part of the Bible, and when I give my evidence, I will take my oath on it.

HAYLEY. Mr. Blake, I must insist that in this matter you take counsel from me! You are my friend, my neighbour: you are doing work for me. Meeting you at my house, people connect us. Also, apart from that, I have a very real affection for you; and I ask you—I must ask you—if this affair comes before the Court, *not* to mention Thomas Paine. Mention Milton if you like: your friendship with Mr. Flaxman, Mr. Stothard, and Mr. Fuseli—all known artists. Mr. Butts too, so long your patron, a man of handsome means and high respectability. But do not go into politics—avoid them! You must realise, my dear Blake, that your politics are not—well, not everybody's politics. The Bench has its prejudices like the Church. I, you know, do not feel bound by what the Church says; I am liberal-minded in my opinions. But when you are before the Bench, you *are* before it. You don't have to go to church ; but you do have to go to court when you are summoned there. And it is so important when there will be prejudice against you, in the fact that you are charged by a soldier with insulting the King's uniform — as I'm afraid you did, Mr. Blake, in throwing it over the gate *twice* — first one and then the other — it is so important that you should make a good impression.

BLAKE. All this trouble, good sir, that you are giving yourself on my behalf, though very kind, is quite unnecessary. The visions tell me not to be afraid ; so you, my friend, need not be afraid either. It will not be necessary, they assure me, to call Tom Paine, or any of my own witnesses ; so I will say nothing except the plain truth as to what happened, and will leave you and any others you may be kind enough to call as to my character to make upon the judge and jury the impression which I am sure they will make. I know, Mr. Hayley, that I have said hasty things, that I have done hasty things ; but life itself is a hasty process, and if one does not catch the moment as it flies it has gone for all eternity. While you have been taking such kind pains to convince me of what I should do, I have been conversing with the spirits of the Eternal Ages — not with any inattention to

what you were saying, I assure you ; for man has
two minds by which he comes to the truth, a
lower and a higher, and these can only act and
become a unity if they agree in the direction of
their aim. So now I am brought to the life of the
senses by the reminder of certain laws of hospi-
tality which go back to the days when Abraham
entertained Angels. I smell roast mutton, and I
see Mrs. Blake looking anxious. Mr. Hayley, will
you honour us ?

> (*But Mr. Hayley, though now of a friendly
> mind, has still his position — and eventu-
> alities — to consider. To share a meal
> with one so recently charged with sedi-
> tion would not be prudent ; and so to
> Mr. Blake on the one side, and to Mrs.
> Blake, standing anxious in the doorway,
> on the other, he makes his polite excuses.*)

HAYLEY. No, indeed, dear Mr. Blake, I thank
you. No, Mrs. Blake, do not trouble ! I have
guests at home, who will be expecting me : it is
almost time I were back. Therefore, you must let
me excuse myself. Roast mutton ? Oh, excellent ! — nothing I like better, had it been possible.
And, my dear Mr. Blake, I don't think you could
have said " Damn the King ! " in *any* circumstances, or with any meaning, however harmless.
Try and think not ! Try and think not ! It would

be so much better—so much safer—to be quite sure that the word "King" was never uttered. The truth, of course; *that* before all things! But—dear Mr. Blake—nothing *but* the truth. *No* political opinions—or names. Oh, promise me; and try to think *not!* Good-bye!

> (*And quite happy in the sense that at least he has made an impression, off he goes to his imaginary guests. Blake stands looking after him, and presently speaks.*)

BLAKE. Oh, why was I born with a different face?
Why was I not born like the rest of my race?
When I look, each one starts: when I speak, I offend.
When silent and passive, I lose my best friend.
Then my verse I dishonour, my pictures despise;
My person degrade, and my temper chastise:
The pen is my terror, the pencil my shame;
All my talents I bury, and dead is my fame.
Here either too low or too highly I'm prized;
When elate I am envied, when meek I'm despised.

Mrs. BLAKE. What's that, Mr. Blake?

BLAKE. My own epitaph, woman! On that part of me which died to-day. The spirits don't like Felpham: they were angry and wanted to get me away. So they sent two Devils—one in a red coat, and the other in a brown—to do it for them.

Never trust appearances, Mrs. Blake. Appearances are the Devil!

MRS. BLAKE. If I was to trust appearances, Mr. Blake, I'd say you in your black coat, tossing 'em across the gate like a mad bull, looked a deal more like the Devil than they did.

BLAKE. Quite right, woman : so I was the Devil to them—and had to be. One has to appear to every man in the form he best comprehends. The Devil is the only good some people can perceive, which is why God allows him to exist. Had I appeared to them more spiritually, they would not have seen me.

MRS. BLAKE. Well, to be sure, that would have surprised them—to be run down the garden and over the gate by something they couldn't see!

BLAKE. If we could all appear to each other as we are in reality, it would be such a new world we should no longer be surprised at anything.

MRS. BLAKE. Well, I'm never surprised at you, Mr. Blake—not now.

BLAKE. That's true, woman-angel ; and a great mercy for both of us.

MRS. BLAKE. (*Concluding.*) I've learned better.

BLAKE. So the visions have decided for us :

London will see us again. Naked we came, naked we shall return—naked, but not ashamed, woman. Aye, Mr. Hayley has meant kindly, I don't doubt —wanted me to wear his old clothes !

MRS. BLAKE. Did he, Mr. Blake ?

BLAKE. I hear a voice you cannot hear, that says I must not stay :

> I see a hand you cannot see, that beckons me away.

MRS. BLAKE. Oh, Mr. Blake, not poetry—dinner, please ! The mutton's getting overdone.

> (*And at that moment Sister Lizzy enters carrying the coat.*)

LIZZY. Here's your coat, William—mended.

BLAKE. (*As he puts it on.*) What do *you* think of Mr. Hayley, woman—after this ?

MRS. BLAKE. Think of him ? I don't think anything of him, Mr. Blake.

BLAKE. Nor did I, till to-day. But now I perceive, in the light he has brought, that he is a messenger from God ; so is the murderous man, so is mutton—messengers all of them !

> (*And they go in where one of God's messengers —a little overdone—is waiting for them.*)

Charles! Charles!

Characters

BENJAMIN ROBERT HAYDON.

WILLIAM WORDSWORTH.

JOHN KEATS.

CHARLES LAMB.

MR. RITCHIE.

MR. MONKHOUSE.

MR. JATHAN.

A MAN SERVANT.

WILLIAM WORDSWORTH
From a painting by R. Hancock (National Portrait Gallery)

Charles! Charles!

December 28th, 1817.

Mr. Jathan is a stranger to London ; and as, with an air of importance, he puts his cloak and hat into the hands of the waiting man-servant, he looks round the large room in which he finds himself, to gather in what kind of abode a famous painter receives his friends. To Mr. Jathan's taste the room seems bare ; but there are large pictures in it, which he supposes, mistakenly, to be good ; he has, however, the support of the artist himself in thinking so. A door to right and to left, a chimney-piece of the Adam period in the centre, under which a bright fire is burning ; an old writing-desk, a few worn and rather dilapidated chairs, a side-table on which after-dinner tea-things have been placed, a shabby carpet straggling across a shabby floor, these items he notes with a superior air (conscious that in his own domicile he has much better), while the servant, temporarily

89

depositing the hat and cloak just anywhere, prepares to go and inform his master.

SERVANT. Yes, sir, Mr. Haydon is still at dinner, sir.

JATHAN. (*Slightly hurt.*) Mr. Haydon *told* me six o'clock.

SERVANT. It's now five minutes to, sir.

JATHAN. Your clock is wrong.

SERVANT. I will tell Mr. Haydon, sir.

JATHAN. You need not. *I* will tell him.

SERVANT. —that you are here, sir.

JATHAN. Ah! Pray do!

> (*Left to himself, Mr. Jathan is in the undivided company of the person he most respects; though it is to pay his respects to another that he is now waiting. In order that he may make a good impression, he begins practising. He has, you may notice, a prophetic resemblance to a certain retired comedian of our judicial Bench, but with more inches to his stature, and less brain. Lifting a long neck, he clears his throat, then speaks :*)

Oh! how do you do, Mr. Wordsworth? So honoured to meet you!

> *(This, however, seems not to satisfy him ; he tries again :)*

No, no—better. Ah ! Mr. Wordsworth ! This meeting. What an honour ! What a privilege !

> *(He is of a mind to try a third time ; but turns to find his rehearsal has been cut short by the entry of his host, Mr. Benjamin Robert Haydon, followed by the servant, who takes up his leavings, and, crossing, retires by the other door. Haydon is a brisk-moving man of forty, with an amiable intelligent face, over-balanced by a large nose ; his head is beginning to be bald. His wear is of the period when there was no sharp dividing-line between the dress which is called "morning" and that which is called "evening"—a suit of respectable black, but by no means smart. Though genial in character, his manner to this guest is a little formal.)*

HAYDON. Pardon me, sir, to have kept you waiting.

JATHAN. *(Generously shaping his grievance.)* It is your clock that is at fault, sir ; not you.

HAYDON. I am afraid we didn't sit down very punctually.

JATHAN. (*Rubbing it in.*) You are still dining ?

HAYDON. No, we have dined. My guests will join us in a moment.

JATHAN. You have Mr. Wordsworth, I hope, with you ?

HAYDON. Why, yes ; Mr. Wordsworth is one of them.

JATHAN. It would have been a disappointment to have come here without meeting Mr. Wordsworth : my reason for coming.

HAYDON. (*Politely accepting this obliterating remark.*) And a very good reason, my dear sir.

JATHAN. My *only* reason.

HAYDON. Well——

> (*And you wonder how he is going to take it ; but the self-wrapt Mr. Jathan continues without pause to display the obtuseness with which God has gifted him.*)

JATHAN. I consider Mr. Wordsworth to be a great genius. Do you not think, sir, that I am right ?

> (*Mr. Jathan's pontifical placing of Wordsworth for his generation makes conversational response a little difficult.*)

92

HAYDON. I ? Well. . . . Ah ! Here they come.

(*The door opens, and three of the guests enter ; but Wordsworth is not among them. The smallest of the three is the most notice-able ; he has obviously dined. As the door opens, he begins talking with a slight stutter.*)

LAMB. Haydon, I tell Wordsworth that if he d-d-drank more he would writer better p-p-poetry.

HAYDON. Where's the proof ? *Your* poetry is not better than his, Charles. Let me introduce you. Mr. . . . ? I'm sorry.

JATHAN. Jathan.

HAYDON. Mr. Jathan, Mr. Charles Lamb.

JATHAN. (*With pomp.*) How do you do, sir ?

LAMB. (*Entirely without it.*) Thank you, I—I—I'm looking rather -- p-p-pale to-day.

JATHAN. I should have said not.

LAMB. You sh-sh-shouldn't have said any-thing !

(*At this Mr. Jathan stiffens his neck in sur-prised annoyance ; but the cause of it, turning his back, has gone to sit by the*

93

fire. Meanwhile two other guests have entered, and Haydon proceeds to do the honours.)

HAYDON. Mr. Jathan — my friends : Mr. Ritchie, Mr. Monkhouse.

MONKHOUSE. Your servant, sir.

RITCHIE. Delighted, I'm sure.

JATHAN. (*Correctively.*) Pray, which is which, sir ?

HAYDON. This is Mr. Ritchie.

JATHAN. (*Making quite sure.*) Oh — Mr. Ritchie.

(*Mr. Jathan's unfortunate air of self-import-ance has roused the enmity of Lamb, who flippantly interjects the first nonsense that occurs to him.*)

LAMB. A m-m-moneylender.

JATHAN. (*Intelligently discovering the obvious.*) Then *you* are — Mr. Monkhouse ?

LAMB. Right !

JATHAN. *Not* Mr. Ritchie. Now I have it.

LAMB. (*Talking into the fire-place, but aiming his remarks elsewhere.*)

94

Oh, it's true, quite true
That twice one's two,
That old's not new,
That black's not blue,
That grog's not glue,
That Sal's not Sue,
That you're not me, and that I'm not you!

RITCHIE. (*Going to him.*) Charles, what's the matter?

LAMB. Matter? Pus; pus! Look at it!

RITCHIE. But you shouldn't call me a money-lender.

LAMB. Why not? You always *are* lending it.

(*The two remaining guests, Mr. Wordsworth
and Mr. John Keats, have now entered
in close conversation, which their host
has to interrupt.*)

HAYDON. Here is Mr. Wordsworth. Wordsworth, this is Mr. Jathan, who has come more than a hundred miles for the chance of meeting you.

WORDSWORTH. (*Bowing.*) I am honoured.

JATHAN. You have a right to be honoured, sir.

(*This does not sound exactly as it is meant,
and elicits from Lamb by the fire a sharp*

95

*squeal of mental torture. But Mr.
Jathan, who has his piece to recite,
flows on in swelling tones.*)

Oh, Mr. Wordsworth! This meeting! What an
honour! What a privilege!

WORDSWORTH. I didn't quite catch your name,
sir?

LAMB. D-don't!

JATHAN. Jathan, sir. To meet you at last!
Your poetry; your genius! I haven't words!

WORDSWORTH. Sometimes I haven't either, Mr.
Jathan. It is a difficulty which all writers experience. Are *you* a writer?

JATHAN. No, sir, no. My duties are official: I
sign. I am a Comptroller of Stamps.

LAMB. (*Beating a tattoo with his feet.*) He can't
control mine!

MONKHOUSE. Sit down, Charles, sit down!

HAYDON. Mr. Jathan—Mr. Keats. He is
another of our poets.

JATHAN. Indeed? I have not heard of you.

(*To which Keats bows his head in fitting
silence.*)

96

LAMB. And I'll be bound he hasn't heard of you, either !

JATHAN. (*Magnificently.*) I beg your pardon, sir ?

LAMB. And you can go on begging it, sir !

WORDSWORTH. Charles ! Charles !

HAYDON. I venture to say you will hear of Mr. Keats, some day, sir.

JATHAN. Well, stranger things have happened — *do* happen.

LAMB. They do ! They stand on their hind legs, and they — br-bray !

WORDSWORTH. My dear Charles !

LAMB. (*To Monkhouse.*) Am I a dream ! Or is *he* ? Do I wake or sleep ?

KEATS. " Do I wake or sleep ? " Thank you, Mr. Lamb. You have finished a poem for me. The words — the very words I was in search of !

LAMB. If *I* could finish *him !*

JATHAN. Has the gentleman been drinking, Mr. Haydon ?

HAYDON. No, no. Mr. Lamb is a humorist. He must have his joke. Pay no attention.

JATHAN. I do not, sir. Mr. Wordsworth, you have come up from the north?

WORDSWORTH. I have, sir. I live in the north.

JATHAN. You have had a long journey.

WORDSWORTH. Yes.

JATHAN. And when you go back, it will be another long journey.

WORDSWORTH. The same distance both ways, sir.

LAMB. Got him!

JATHAN. You find that the landscape of the Lake District conduces to the production of poetry, Mr. Wordsworth?

LAMB. Ah, God!

    (*But Mr. Jathan is not to be diverted from his thirst for knowledge.*)

JATHAN. It does, does it not?

WORDSWORTH. More perhaps than London, as a *rule*.

JATHAN. So I should suppose.

WORDSWORTH. Though on Westminster Bridge I did break it on one occasion.

JATHAN. On Westminster Bridge ? You surprise me ! For the Bridge — what an honour !

(*At this point Lamb rises in an attitude of visionary recitation.*)

LAMB. Is this a dagger that I see before me, the handle toward my hand ? Come, let me clutch it !

(*He makes a grab at Mr. Jathan, who retreats. Monkhouse and Ritchie seize hold of Lamb and drag him back to his seat, Lamb continuing meanwhile :*)

I have thee not, and yet I see thee still !
Out, out damned spot !

(*They almost have to sit on him to bring the recitation to a conclusion ; and he continues to form a restive background to the dialogue which follows, with Monkhouse at hand to keep him in order.*)

HAYDON. (*Tactfully, for a diversion.*) Well ? and how did the argument resolve itself in the other room ? Any conclusion ?

KEATS. Our main conclusion — agreement (at least, Mr. Lamb agreed to it for us) — was that Newton deserved hanging as a murderer for having dissected the rainbow into prismatic colours.

99

HAYDON. But why not ?

RITCHIE. Had Wordsworth done that, he could never have written his poem.

WORDSWORTH. Well, but Newton *has* done it ; and I have written my poem ; and the rainbow hasn't suffered.

LAMB. Oh, hasn't it ! Nobody can ever look at a rainbow now, Wordsworth, without thinking of you. What could be worse ?

RITCHIE. Why, Newton would be worse ; you said so.

LAMB. Newton ? Newton is dead mutton. Wordsworth's alive ; a walking infection ! You can't hear a cuckoo now ; it's the wandering voice of Wordsworth. You can't say " We are seven " — as we are now — but, it's Wordsworth and "brother Jim " counting the tombstones. Wordsworth's a murderer, if you like !

JATHAN. Really, sir, I don't think your argument is sound.

LAMB. No ; but it's sense.

JATHAN. (*Valiant for truth.*) Mr. Wordsworth is not a murderer in any sense of the word.

LAMB. It would be sound sense if I murdered *you*, sir.

JATHAN. I don't follow you, I fear.

LAMB. No, I should follow you—at the rope's end. But if the jury knew *you*, they'd acquit me.

MONKHOUSE. Charles, come and sit over here and talk to me.

HAYDON. But how did Newton come in ?

WORDSWORTH. Really, I even forget now how the discussion started.

RITCHIE. Why, it started in Lamb saying that you said Voltaire was dull. You said again he *was* dull. Then the question arose what made people dull—what made things dull. Somebody said that Milton's deity was dull ; and I said that Newton's rainbow was dull when he reduced it to prismatic colours. Whereupon Charles called him a murderer.

JATHAN. But pardon me, sir : was not Newton a great genius ?

LAMB. Eh ? What's that ?

MONKHOUSE. Sh ! Sh !

> (*While Ritchie was speaking, the servant has brought in and poured out tea, and now stands at the elbow of an unobservant guest, waiting to hand it. This enables Haydon once more to effect a diversion.*)

HAYDON. Will you take your tea, gentlemen?

(*The servant goes round offering it, Jathan alone declines.*)

WORDSWORTH. Mr. Keats, I have not thanked you yet for sending me your poem.

KEATS. I thank *you*, Mr. Wordsworth, for reading it : if you did, sir.

WORDSWORTH. I read it, yes, I read it. The *Hymn to Pan* I admired ; a very pretty pagan conceit. But do you, Mr. Keats, believe in Pan?

KEATS. Do not you, sir?

WORDSWORTH. Not Pan in that sense ; no.

KEATS. But a Pan of the senses, surely! In all your poetry, sir, you make sense the very basis of spiritual conception—feeling—imagination.

WORDSWORTH. But I don't give it an imaginary body.

KEATS. But to believe in it, we must! Christianity had to give itself belief in a body—else it would not have conquered the world.

WORDSWORTH. And if Christianity dies, it will be because belief in that body can no longer be what it was.

KEATS. That is what I am saying, sir.

WORDSWORTH. No, you were not saying it, Mr. Keats.

KEATS. I was meaning it.

WORDSWORTH. Then perhaps you agree with me more than I wholly realised. I hope you do. I note that Milton influences you. Be careful. Also Shakespeare : the Shakespearean form of the sonnet has your allegiance. Yes ; but be on your guard. I could have written like Shakespeare, had I had a mind.

LAMB. Yes ; it was the m-mind that was l-lacking.

WORDSWORTH. It was, Charles, it was. I've a very good mind of my own.

LAMB. Worthy Wordy !

KEATS. I appreciate what you say about Milton, sir : for myself I have found him to be a danger.

(*At this Mr. Jathan opens his eyes disapprovingly.*)

HAYDON. Mr. Jathan, you are not taking any tea.

JATHAN. No, sir ; I was occupied in listening — to Mr. Wordsworth. Pray, sir, do you not think that Milton was a great genius ?

LAMB. Eh ? What's that ?

(*Jathan gives him a silent stare.*)

Did I hear you say, sir, that Milton was a great genius ?

JATHAN. No, sir. I asked Mr. Wordsworth if he were not.

LAMB. Oh ! Then you are a silly fellow !

WORDSWORTH. Charles ! my dear Charles !

JATHAN. (*Magnificently ignoring the rudeness.*) Indeed, sir, is it not correct to say that Milton and Newton were *both* great geniuses ?

(*Lamb, seizing a candle from the chimney-piece, advances toward Mr. Jathan, with phrenological intent.*)

LAMB. Will you allow me, sir, to look at your b-b-bumps ?

WORDSWORTH. Charles ! Charles !

HAYDON. You are dropping the wax about, Charles. Put it down !

(*Lamb is persuaded back to his chair, and the candle is taken from him.*)

WORDSWORTH. Genius, my dear sir, exists in

various degrees. In some cases it is so obvious one has not to mention it.

JATHAN. Why, of course, sir ; that is so. In your own case, it would be quite superfluous to——

LAMB. Diddle-diddle, dumpling, my son John
      Went to bed with his b-b-breeches on !

WORDSWORTH. Charles, Charles !

HAYDON. Did I hear you and Keats just now discussing theology ?

WORDSWORTH. Dismissing it, rather. The theology of classic time, expounded in modern verse, is merely a curiosity.

KEATS. But when you wrote *Laodamia*, sir, you yourself took a classic subject, and brought in the gods.

WORDSWORTH. Why, yes, for a moral purpose, by way of illustration.

KEATS. Is not all life illustration, sir ?

JATHAN. Pardon me, sir ; I have in my library many lives that are without illustration.

LAMB. Diddle-diddle dumpling, my son John.

JATHAN. (*Continuing, without waiting for this ebullition to end.*) Would it not be more correct to say that life was the result of experience ?

LAMB. Went to bed with his b-b-breeches on !

WORDSWORTH. I should be more inclined to say
that experience was the result of life. In your own
life, Mr. —— (*he paused*).

JATHAN. Jathan, sir. I apprehend that you do
not remember me, Mr. Wordsworth ?

WORDSWORTH. Indeed ; I am unfortunate.

JATHAN. Yet I have had the honour of corre-
sponding with you.

WORDSWORTH. With me ? Not that I remember.

JATHAN. You do not, sir ? I am Comptroller of
Stamps over your own district, Mr. Wordsworth —
a Government appointment of some importance,
I venture to think.

LAMB. A damned foolish Government !

JATHAN. And I have myself supplied you with
stamps. An honour.

LAMB. Hey diddle-diddle !
      The cat and the fiddle !

WORDSWORTH. My dear Charles !

MONKHOUSE. (*Aside to Ritchie.*) We must get
him out of this, or there will be murder !

KEATS. What a subject for a poem!

LAMB. Eh? What subject!

KEATS. Dissection of your victim into his original prismatic colours, Mr. Lamb.

LAMB. Blood!

>   (*The servant who has again been going round, attending to his duties, passes across at this moment.*)

HAYDON. Surely, Mr. Jathan, a little tea? Now others are having more.

JATHAN. In Mr. Wordsworth's company, sir, one can hardly descend to such a thing as tea.

LAMB. Upon my word and conscience,
>   How such a thing can be!
> We descend to talking nonsense,
>   But we don't descend to tea!

HAYDON. Charles, come into the other room. I want you and Monkhouse to tell me what you think of some of my pictures.

LAMB. Do let me have another look at the gentleman's bumps.

MONKHOUSE. No, Charles; come and see the pictures.

LAMB. The b-b-b-bumps first!

MONKHOUSE. What's the use ? You can't change them. Now criticise Haydon's pictures and he can——

LAMB. But he won't !

(*He leads him away. They still hear him.*)

HAYDON. Ritchie, go in and help Monkhouse to keep him quiet. I must stay here.

> (*Ritchie goes out with the other two ; and the door closes behind them ; but Lamb continues to be audible, he goes on preferring the bumps to the pictures.*)

JATHAN. I don't think, sir, that Mr. Lamb likes me.

HAYDON. (*Apologetically.*) Oh, but why think that ?

JATHAN. Does he usually behave — like that — to people he likes ?

HAYDON. After dinner he behaves anyhow. We take no notice.

JATHAN. It is rather difficult *not* to take notice.

HAYDON. Yes ; till you are accustomed to him.

JATHAN. He is a friend of yours, sir ?

HAYDON. Why, yes.

JATHAN. (*To Wordsworth.*) And a friend of yours, sir ?

WORDSWORTH. Yes ; a great friend.

JATHAN. That, I confess, surprises me.

KEATS. He is a continual surprise to everyone who knows him, Mr. Jathan. That is part of his charm.

> (*At this moment the voice of Lamb is heard again :* " I want to see his b-b-bumps ! " *This gives Mr. Jathan just the material he requires.*)

JATHAN. " Charm," sir, did you say ?

KEATS. I said " charm."

JATHAN. A word somewhat difficult to define, don't you think ?

KEATS. Perhaps ; but easy to recognise when met.

JATHAN. (*Sententiously.*) Oh.

HAYDON. (*Making conversation.*) More easy, one might say, than the recognition of genius.

> (*This starts Mr. Jathan off once more on his favourite topic. The servant re-enters, places a spirit stand and glasses, and retires again.*)

JATHAN. (*To Wordsworth.*) And who would you name, sir, as the greatest genius that ever lived ?

> (*The door opens ; a portion of Lamb is seen struggling in the arms of his friends : his voice is heard :* " I want to see that fellow's b-b-bumps ! " *The door shuts again.*)

WORDSWORTH. Really, Mr, Jathan, that is a matter I never thought of deciding. It lies beyond me — beyond any of us.

JATHAN. Indeed, Mr. Wordsworth, you surprise me !

WORDSWORTH. For all we know, the works of the greatest genius no longer exist — are lost to us.

JATHAN. But is not that contrary to a belief in Providence ?

WORDSWORTH. That is arguable, sir.

JATHAN. I would not presume to argue with you, Mr. Wordsworth : you are a man of genius. But I believe in Providence. (*To Haydon.*) Do not you believe in Providence, sir ?

HAYDON. (*Devoutly.*) I do. I do.

JATHAN. (*To Keats.*) And you, sir ?

KEATS. I have an open mind on the subject,

Mr. Jathan. But if it was Providence which made us all meet here this evening, I think it was a blind Providence.

JATHAN. A blind Providence ? That is a contradiction in terms, sir.

KEATS. Then let us leave it at that.

WORDSWORTH. Yes, Mr. Jathan, let us leave it at that.

HAYDON. No ; pardon me ! Providence may be blind — inattentive to small events. But through the great minds of genius I hold that Providence has eyes.

KEATS. But not the same eyes, Mr. Haydon. They all see differently.

WORDSWORTH. Then what they see is not the truth. Truth is all one ; to see rightly, one must know it.

KEATS. But poets see so much more than they know, Mr. Wordsworth. If they wrote only what they knew, half the poetry in the world would never have been written.

WORDSWORTH. Poetry which the world could spare.

KEATS. Ah, no, sir ! The world ? Well, *I* can't

speak for it ; only for myself. But if Milton had kept only to what he *knew* he could never have written *Paradise Lost*. Surely a poet writes not as he knows, but as he feels.

WORDSWORTH. But not *all* he feels, Mr. Keats. Feeling may become licentious.

KEATS. Even licentious feeling has produced great poetry, sir.

WORDSWORTH. That I should be inclined to deny.

KEATS. Then you must close the classics, sir ; and Sappho must no longer be named. Surely the good things of this world are mixed.

WORDSWORTH. Aye : but there are some which won't mix. I should doubt the results if you tried to rewrite a poem of mine, Mr. Keats ; or I one of yours.

KEATS. Yet I have rewritten some of my own poems *because* of you, sir. You can put a pot on the fire, without putting the fire *into* the pot.

WORDSWORTH. That is a very just remark, Mr. Keats. I like talking with you, even though we do not agree.

JATHAN. But though Mr. Keats does not agree with you, sir, *I* do !

(At this there is an awful pause : none of the others are capable of saying anything. Through the door the voice of Lamb comes to the rescue.

LAMB. (*From within.*) What ? Hasn't the fellow gone yet ?

JATHAN. (*Rising.*) I fear, sir, I am causing your friend some impatience, and I notice that it grows late. Therefore, I think I must be going.

HAYDON. (*Not very pressingly.*) Oh, won't you stay a little longer ? There will be supper presently.

JATHAN. I thank you, no. I am infinitely obliged for this opportunity, this privilege, which you have allowed me. A most interesting occasion, I venture to think. Do not you also think it has been a most interesting occasion?

HAYDON. The interest, I am sure, sir, has been shared by all of us.

JATHAN. Mr. Wordsworth (*bowing over his hand*), a red-letter day in my life ; a meeting that I shall never forget.

WORDSWORTH. Very good of you to say so, I'm sure. Good night.

JATHAN. Good night, sir. (*Then to Keats.*) Good night, sir. (*To Haydon.*) Good night . . . Oh, but don't let me trouble you !

H

HAYDON. (*Politely getting rid of him.*) Pray let me see you to the door.

    (*As they pass out, Jathan's ejaculations are still heard.*)·

JATHAN. Ah, no! Remain, remain! You have Mr. Wordsworth with you.

    (*The door closes. There is a pause. The two poets look at each other.*)

WORDSWORTH. Well, well!——Well!

KEATS. "Well"? I wish I had your vision, Mr. Wordsworth. I wish I could feel——*well.*

    (*The inner door opens. Monkhouse puts in a cautious head.*)

MONKHOUSE. Gone? May we come in again?

    (*And without waiting for further permission they do, Lamb looking about him very suspiciously to make sure that the enemy has really cleared off.*)

WORDSWORTH. Charles, you behaved abominably!

LAMB. S-s-someone had to. If I hadn't—you all would.

WORDSWORTH. Yes; but you know, Charles, you'd been drinking—too much.

LAMB. Wordie, dear, we'd all been drinking. But for that, we shouldn't have survived.

(Haydon re-enters. Lamb goes to spirit-stand and helps himself.)

HAYDON. Oh, really, really! Dear me! I do apologise to everybody!

LAMB. Why should you? God made him: *you* didn't.

HAYDON. He invited himself, and I let him come.

KEATS. Blind Providence!

HAYDON. Oh, but the man's beyond words!

MONKHOUSE. Then why talk of him?

RITCHIE. Mr. Wordsworth, what do you say?

WORDSWORTH. An experience, Ritchie; an experience.

LAMB. G-g-gentlemen, I p-p-propose a toast! The death of Jathan; and may he go to h-h-h-heaven, and be changed.

RITCHIE. In the twinkling of an eye, let's hope.

LAMB: *His* eye won't twinkle — ever, Ritchie.

WORDSWORTH. I don't like drinking to the death of any man.

LAMB. It's the only way sometimes. You can't abolish capital punishment for everything. Jathan is an unforgivable crime. May his father be forgiven! But I doubt it. *(Drinks.)* Jathan, Jathan! go where you are — not wanted.

MONKHOUSE. (*Taking Lamb by the arm.*) I think I had better make Charles say good night, Haydon ; and many, many——

HAYDON. Oh, but you are not going yet !

LAMB. Going ? Yes : we are all going. Bed, every one ! Worthy Wordie, dear, don't write a poem about Jathan. If you do I shall turn atheist.

MONKHOUSE. Come along, come along !

> (*Monkhouse manipulates him tenderly to the door ; Lamb clings to it for a moment, giving his best imitation of Wordsworth, as a farewell offering :*)

LAMB. " Charles ! Charles ! "——Good night !

KEATS. I think I am spiritually called, Haydon. It looks as though Monkhouse would have more than he can manage. Good-bye, and thanks. I will send that poem. Mr. Wordsworth, your advice I shall remember and value ; but I shall go on believing in Pan. Good-bye.

> (*The other two have gone. Keats follows. There is a moment's silence. Then, in a tone of wise philosophy, Wordsworth speaks.*)

WORDSWORTH. Humanity ! What a mystery ! What incredible examples of it we do meet !

HAYDON. I'm very sorry, my dear Wordsworth,

that I let him come at all. The fellow was impossible!

WORDSWORTH. No, no, no. I wasn't thinking of that self-crowned flea. Self? Is it his own doing? If a flea is under a king's crown at the moment of his coronation, I suppose the flea is crowned with him. That's the world as God made it! No; it was Charles I meant.

HAYDON. Charles can't suffer fools gladly.

WORDSWORTH. No; but he helps us to. It's a great gift, Haydon—a very spiritual gift. To-night he behaved abominably; but he's the best man I know.

RITCHIE. Charles is a saint.

HAYDON. Not a calendar-saint, I'm afraid.

WORDSWORTH. No; of the new faith which has yet to come.

RITCHIE. And to what shall we pray, when we belong to it?

WORDSWORTH. We shall be the prayers.

RITCHIE. Praying—to ourselves?

WORDSWORTH. Aye; for others. People will always love Charles—always, as long as names are remembered. Will they love *me*?

RITCHIE. Do you think they will pray to him?

WORDSWORTH. No; as I said, he will himself be the prayer.

HAYDON. That's a curious thought, Wordsworth. You know, I'm not sure that you are a Christian. I heard you talking to Keats about Christianity. You shouldn't say things like that to a young man.

WORDSWORTH. Keats is not a young man if he is an immortal.

RITCHIE. What do you think of his poetry?

WORDSWORTH. I? Well; perhaps I am not to judge. Talent, great talent; but to what is he devoting it? An outworn creed. Will it live?

RITCHIE. Why not? Don't we still hanker after the outworn creeds, Wordsworth? —
" for glimpses that would make us less forlorn :
 Have sight of Proteus rising from the sea,
 Or hear old Triton blow his wreathèd horn."

WORDSWORTH. Yes, yes. Well, if the net of poetry is as wide as that of St. Peter — clean, and unclean, we are all in it : not to be called common. Good night, Haydon.

HAYDON. Good night, Wordsworth; it has been a delight to see you again.

WORDSWORTH. The entertainment was perfect.

HAYDON. Very good of you to say so.

RITCHIE. I think, I also, must be saying——

HAYDON. No, no, Ritchie ; don't go ! I want to speak to you for just one moment.

RITCHIE. Then I must say good-bye now, Wordsworth.

WORDSWORTH. Good-bye ? You start on your travels — when ?

RITCHIE. In three days.

> (*The voices of Haydon and Wordsworth are heard still as they disappear. Left alone, Ritchie stands looking at one of the great pictures which cover the walls. But his look is gloomy ; he shakes his head : he does not admire it. Haydon returns.*)

HAYDON. Aye, look at it, Ritchie ! There is fame waiting for me : fame — and fortune.

RITCHIE. The hope helps you, I suppose ?

HAYDON. Aye ; but without the certainty that one was creating art — art which will never die, hope would be empty.

RITCHIE. You wanted to speak to me.

HAYDON. Ritchie, I'm in great temporary difficulty. Will you lend me——

RITCHIE. My dear Haydon, I've lent you all I can afford. I'm sorry — I am in debt myself.

HAYDON. I am not merely in debt. I shall be in the Fleet to-morrow if I don't pay. (*He moves away*.) I won't press you. (*A pause*.)

RITCHIE. How much ?

HAYDON. Thirty pounds odd.

RITCHIE. And then ? Will that clear you ?

HAYDON. In a month both my other great pictures will be finished.

RITCHIE. Yes—— You've done ten. How many have you sold ?

HAYDON. Three. But I have had offers for all.

RITCHIE. What kind of offers ?

HAYDON. Ridiculous offers, insulting offers, dishonest, calculating offers ! These Jew money-lenders know that in ten years my work will be famous and sought after all the world over. Ritchie, I know what I'm talking about. My countrymen are slow to recognise genius ; they always have been. But in the end they do. I shall live, Ritchie, I shall live ! " Benjamin Robert

120

Haydon " ; can you hear the sound of that name —
and believe it is a name that will perish ? And
between me and the great destiny that awaits me
for the establishing of that name — what stands ?
Just this miserable need of thirty pounds. God !
Think of it ?

RITCHIE. You didn't try your friend the Comptroller of Stamps, I suppose ?

HAYDON. He is not my friend. We had only
corresponded. Till he came to me to-day and
begged for this introduction, I had never seen
him. No, Ritchie, him I did not ask !

RITCHIE. Since you deal even with money-
lenders, I wonder why not.

HAYDON. I wonder that you suggest it !

RITCHIE. Because he would have paid for the
introduction.

HAYDON. (*Magnificently.*) I don't sell my
friends, Ritchie.

RITCHIE. (*Drily.*) It comes cheaper than bor-
rowing of them.

HAYDON. Do you doubt my repaying you ?

RITCHIE. I don't doubt your intention of repaying me, Haydon.

HAYDON. If you did not believe in my genius, Ritchie : if I did not believe in it myself, as surely as I believe in God, the God who gave it me, I would not ask you for a penny.

RITCHIE. You would not ? No ; I am sure of it.

HAYDON. Aye, as surely as the sun will rise to-morrow, so surely, some day, my sun will rise, and my name will be remembered as a creator of the Art !

RITHCIE. Well, Haydon, you are a man of faith. Faith is said to move mountains. You have moved *me*. I will see what I can do—— Good night.

> (*He gives Haydon his hand, with good-will, but without either enthusiasm or conviction. Haydon, too much moved to speak, presses it, and lets him go. Then, finding himself alone, he resumes that measure of a man, which is an angel, which he so devoutly believes to be his.*)

HAYDON. Aye ! And the world shall see what *I* can do. Listen to me, you forms, created, conceived, begotten, emanations of my brain ! This hand has made you eternal. Yet there you stand knowing nothing of it all. But the world shall know. God, would'st thou have allowed me to be born with such fire in me, merely that it should fade out and die ?

(*The man-servant enters.*)

SERVANT. Oh, I beg pardon, sir. Have all the gentlemen gone ?

HAYDON. Yes, John ; you may lock up. I will put out the lights.

(*John takes a tray and goes.*)

Well, what time is it ? (*Looks at clock.*) Ah ! my diary ! I must write up my diary, before I forget. (*He sits and begins to get out writing materials.*) A wonderful evening ! What an experience !—— " Let me look at the gentleman's bumps." " Charles ! Charles ! "

> (*He chuckles ; his face becomes quite happy, forgetting his troubles, forgetting himself, forgetting his huge self-deception in that matter of his own genius, he sits writing the diary which is destined to outlive all his other creations in art.*)

The Cutty Stool

Characters

ROBERT BURNS.

ANDREW PATON.

A MINISTER.

TWO ELDERS.

ROBERT BURNS
From a painting by Alexander Nasmyth (National Portrait Gallery)

The Cutty Stool

1784.

It is a Sunday morning late in November in the year of our Lord, 1784, when Mauchline Kirk, unaware of the honour that has befallen it, takes its since-recognised place in the historical comedy of man's making of man.

In the gaunt, white-washed interior we see the front end of a seated congregation, facing (across an empty space of floor backed by a blank wall with a door leading out) the high-decked pulpit which stands opposite. The windows are too high up to admit a view, but they cannot conceal the fact that outside is a fine day.

The pulpit is energetically occupied by an elderly minister in a black gown. Before him, on the book-rest, sleeps a large Bible — closed, that is to say. But the thumpings it endures would surely rouse to protest anything which had in it as much of the spirit of truth as was in Balaam's ass when it opened its mouth to complain against unjust thwackings. On this occasion, however, no miracle happens ; and the prophet is left to have his own way.

Below the book-rest, and sufficiently away to prevent the leaning-back of its occupant, stands the cutty-stool ; and the fact that to-day it is occupied by Robert Burns will, at a future date, make it so sentimentally valuable both to the Scottish nation, who still read him, and the English, who still pretend to, that an honoured place would be found for it— if not in Westminster Abbey, in any other shrine of national self-worship one likes to name. Robert Burns is sitting with his back to the minister ; and that, perhaps, is as well, for the expression of his face is not attentive. And though one might charitably assume, from his absorbed demeanour and bent head, that thought had gone inwards, carrying the minister's word with it, and separating him from consciousness of outward things—even of the inquisitorial eyes of his neighbours here directed against him row behind row— there is now and then a stealthy movement of the hand covered by the bonnet upon his knee, which suggests mental occupation of another kind.

The service proper is over ; and the address, whose peroration we now hear, is being delivered entirely for the benefit of the culprit upon the cutty-stool, *and for the warning of others who may be similarly tempted. And there is this to the good about it, that, under this stark régime of church-discipline, adultery is frankly spoken of and denounced, and is not relegated to its place in the accustomed recital of the Ten Commandments, where for most ears it means nothing. So now the Church has had her say about it ; and, furnished with a selected example for chapter and verse, the word is made flesh and has a meaning, while to a properly scandalised congregation the minister thus concludes his remarks :*

MINISTER. Aweel, ma brethren ! an' when ye're a' deed an' damned, ye will look up tae Him frae yer infinite torment an' say " O Lord, why are we here ? " An' God, explaining Hissel' tae the sinner —reasonable as well as just—'ull look down at ye in His infinite mercy and say " For yer sins ! " An' ye'll look up at Him again, frae that infinite torment which'll ever be finding fresh ways to get at ye, an' ye'll say " But, Lord, we didna ken ! We didna ken ! " An' God, in His infinite mercy, 'ull look down at ye again, an' say "Aweel ! ye ken it noo ! "

> *(As the spoken Word of divinely chosen dialect is thus vouched for, the written Word receives a hard knock ; and a rhetorical pause follows.)*

An' ye will, ma brethren, ye will ken it; an' yer lie will hae fun' ye oot! For here hae ye been telt a' aboot it this day, an' been gi'en the good Scripture word for it, so that hereafter ye shall hae nae excuse to yer sins. An' though, like enough, ye'll forget it—an', mind me, some of ye will!—ye ken it noo! So dinna say the Lord hasna gi'en ye yer chance, ye writhing worms, ye miserable blind moles, ye hopping, skipping hypocrites! For A've told it tae a' o' ye; an' hae shown ye the road ye're gaun—the broad road that leadeth tae destruction. An' there A see ye running doon it, tae right an' tae left, wi' a foot in each ditch—sae fond o' it, ye think ye canna' hae too muckle o' it. But ye will; for ye'll hae it to a' eternity—a road withoot end.

> (*And now from the general he turns to the particular, and with downward-directed gaze adapts the tone of his oratory to the domestic concern which lies immediately before him.*)

An' here's a sinner sitting before ye, snatched back one merciful meenut frae that road he was linking alang sae nimbly, when the Kirk took haud o' him by his hairy scalp that was gaun on still in wickedness, an' told him tae sit here an' repent o' his wrong-doings.

Robert Burns, ye ken why ye're here. An' ye

ken ye've done wrang. For if ye hadna done wrang ye wouldna' be here. An' wi' the eyes o' this congregation upon ye, ye sit an' ye're ashamed. An' they dae weel sae to sit an' look at ye ; an' ye dae weel to be ashamed. But they dinna see ye as God sees ye. He's got an Eye like a gimlet, that pierces to the joints o' yer harness, an' the marrow o' yer bones, an' the trembling jeely o' yer heart—which should a' rin doon tae yer boots, A'm thinking, if ye kent, as A ken, the peril that ye stand in.

But if ye repent it can come up again—only no' too fast, mind ye ! just a wee bit at a time, search-ing itsel' as it comes. Ye've been a sinner wi' women, Robert Burns ; oft times ye've been that, an' we not knowing it. But yer sin wi' ae woman, weak an' wilful like yersel, has fun' ye oot. For the crying o' a bairn born o' sin ye canna cover up wi' a saucepan lid ; ye canna mak' a lamb's stew o' it, nor a pig's hash ! It's got tae come oot ! An' it has come oot ; an' there it is ; and here ye are. An' here A'm telling this congregation that, if ye dinna repent and turn frae yer wicked ways, there'll be a Robbie Burns in Hell, burning like his ain name tae a' eternity ; like yer ain name, Robbie Burns, a red blazing licht for the Deil tae read names by—for a' eternity ! Ye puir miserable sinner, the Lord bless this day tae ye, and mak guid come o' it, though we see it no' !

An' noo, Brethren, we will a' gae oot, an' leave him tae his ain thochts, so that, when he comes tae himsel' again, he may hae the fatted calf killed for him, better than the husks trodden by the feet o' swine. . . . "Amen ! Amen ! An' Amen ! " say a' of ye : then ye can go.

> (*With a murmured confusion of tongues, the congregation makes the required response. There is a preparatory shuffling of feet, which ceases as the minister resumes speaking.*)

Ane o' the Elders will noo collect frae the penitent the usual thank-offering.

> (*An Elder, who has been sitting prepared, comes forward, carrying the bag, which having presented, he stands waiting. And while the Minister proceeds to give out notice of Church-business, Robert Burns sits searching his pocket for the requisite coin ; and the following brief colloquy ensues :*)

BURNS. Mon, hoo muckle is't ?

ELDER. Ye should hae had it ready.

BURNS. So A hae, when ye tell me.

ELDER. It's a guinea.

BURNS. Losh !

> (*Reluctantly the guinea is produced and handed over. And meanwhile, above their heads, the Minister is talking.*)

MINISTER. There will be a meeting for prayer in this place o' worship on Wednesday evening next, at six o'clock, in preparation for the election o' new Elders. The list o' names will be on the kirk-door ; an' ye can read them as ye gae oot.

> (*This concludes matters. The Minister retires through a door behind the pulpit ; and the Elder, carrying the bag of offertory, mounts and goes after him. The congregation, dilatory with curiosity, is now filtering out back and front. An Elder, pausing in his exit, approaches the still-seated occupant of the cutty-stool.*)

ELDER. Ye dinna look penitent, Robbie ; no' as penitent as A would like ye to look.

BURNS. Eh ; but it's a sair thing to be fun' oot, mon ! A'm penitent enough for that. An' you'd be as penitent as me, if A telt 'em a' A' ken aboot ye !

ELDER. Ah ! ye've the Deil in ye still, Robbie.

BURNS. Chained up as a watchdog, to scare awa' shady characters. . . . He's driven ye awa' for ane.

(*The Elder has not waited to hear the end of that retort; he goes out with a snarl, slamming the door. And now, for a moment, the penitent thinks he is alone; when up from the back pews comes a man of his own class, rather younger than himself, friendly, shy, a little awkward —doubtful, perhaps, in what sort of mood he will find his friend after public penance. But this is one whom, for special, though illegitimate, reasons, Burns is glad to get word with. Nevertheless, proudly suspicious, he waits, and it is Andrew Paton, brother to the partner of his present disgrace, who speaks first.*)

ANDREW. Weel, Robbie ?

BURNS. Weel, Andy ?

ANDREW. Are ye na' coming awa' ? Hae ye no' wearied o' yer long sitting yet ?

BURNS. A'm letting it sink in, mon.

ANDREW. Letting what ?

BURNS. Ma repentance. An' A'm waiting till a'

134

the holy anes hae tired o' biding tae see me come oot.

ANDREW. That means that ye're ashamed, then. Ye said ye wouldna' be.

BURNS. Ashamed ? Ye can mak ony mon ashamed by pulling his breeks aff. Yet there was a mony o' 'em to-day — aye, elders, too ! — peering behind what had stooled me, licking their cree-shie fat chaps, an' wishing it had been them — so long as they werena' caught for it ! A had but to look, an' their breeks were a' aff every mon jack o' them.

> (*This outburst had been caused by the return from the vestry of the Elder that had the bag. The attack is direct ; he flies before it. Burns laughs triumphantly.*)

ANDREW. Robbie, ye're awfu' !

BURNS. A am that, Andy. Where do ye come frae ?

ANDREW. Hame : cam' back last nicht.

BURNS. Eh ? Hae ye seen Lizzie ?

ANDREW. A was waiting to tell ye.

BURNS. Hoo is she ?

ANDREW. Oh, doing weel.

BURNS. Ye've seen her ?

ANDREW. Of course A've seen her.

(*But there is something in hand to which at this moment the other's attention is suddenly diverted. Andrew looks on, puzzled.*)

What are ye writing there ?

BURNS. Only the last line.

ANDREW. O' what ?

BURNS. Just thochts that cam tae me the while.

ANDREW. (*Properly scandalised.*) Hae ye been writing it *here* ?

BURNS. Aye.

ANDREW. A' the time ; while everybody was keeking at ye, and Minister preaching ?

BURNS. When else ? They wadna' leave aff ; nor wad he.

ANDREW. (*Dubious.*) What is it, Robbie : a confession ?

BURNS. (*With relish.*) Aye !

ANDREW. Are ye going to mak it public ?

BURNS. Aye ! print it in a book, some day. An'

Scotland's going to sing it for me. Whisky, an' haggis, an' ma songs, Andy, are going tae keep Scotland prood of hersel'.

ANDREW. Yer songs 'ull hae tae be mighty guid, Robbie, tae stand such company.

BURNS. They are, mon! Hark tae this noo! Sit doon!

> (*Robbie rises for the recitation, and Andy sits down in his place, where, before long, his face becomes a picture of contending emotions.*)

BURNS. There's nought but care on every han',
>> In every hour that passes :
>> What signifies the life o' man,
>>> An' 'twere na for the lasses ?
>> Green grow the rashes, O :

Andy, Chorus !

> (*An invocation to which Andy does not respond. Burns gives it alone.*)
>> Green grow the rashes, O ;
>> The sweetest hours that e'er I spend,
>> Are spent among the lasses, O.

ANDREW. (*Scared.*) Oh, Robbie, you mauna' say that in a kirk !

BURNS. Where else better, if it's true ? Haud yer blether !

137

(And he continues.)

> Gie me a cannie hour at e'en,
>> My arms aboot my dearie, O ;
> An' war'ly cares an' war'ly men
>> May a' gae tapsalteerie, O ;
> For you sae douce, ye sneer at this ;
>> Ye're nought but senseless asses, O :
> The wisest mon the warl' e'er saw,
>> He dearly loved the lasses, O.

(King Solomon that was, Andy.)

ANDREW. (*Rising, his sense of desecration too much for him.*) Robbie, ye're just awfu' !

BURNS. A'm just mesel'. Aye, it's awfu' tae be that, is't na' ?

ANDREW. An' ye tae be making that while the Minister was calling ye tae repent o' ye sins !

BURNS. Mon, A had tae get ma mind aff him, else A should 'a howked wi' laughter at a' the foolishness he was telling.

ANDREW. How hae ye remembered it a' ?

BURNS. Wrote it into ma hat, like a hen sits placing her egg, saying naething. But she cackles when it's ower. Is't na' a beautiful poem, Andy ? An' is't na' a' true ? Is't na' God's truth ? Ye ken it weel, Andy. Be honest !

ANDREW. There's some truths ought na' tae be said in kirk, Robbie.

BURNS. For instance ?

ANDREW. A'll no say it — here.

BURNS. Put yer head oot yonder, an' say it loud enough, an' A'll hear it.

ANDREW. Ye come oot, Robbie !

> (*The more to tempt him he now holds out a letter.*)

BURNS. What hae ye got there ? — For me ?

ANDREW. She's sent ye this line.

> (*Burns snatches, and sits down to read it.*)

BURNS. (*Suspiciously.*) Wha wrote it ?

ANDREW. A did ; but they're her ain words as she telt me.

BURNS. (*Reading.*) Aye ; they read like it. . . . Is't a fine bairn ?

ANDREW. It's yer ain image, Robbie.

BURNS. Then it maun be ! (*He sits thinking ; then — his voice changing to tenderness.*) Puir brat ! Puir wee innocent brat ! Where did the making o' bastards come in, A wonder ? A lang time after the making o' mon, sae A reckon. (*Then, challeng-ingly.*) An' that's the ditch yer holy anes will never get ower.

ANDREW. What's that ye say ?

BURNS. If ye put a nightcap on top o' a hill, will that send it to sleep — or a volcano, either ? Or if ye put a piece o' sticking-plaster over the mouth of a river, will that stop the tide running ? There's a mon been inventing a steam-engine, A'm telt ; a very simple true thing, by the sound o' it. Ye fit a cap to its nozzle, an' screw doon till it bursts ; or if it disna burst, it gets up an' does something. That's human nature, Andy. It's a great dis-covery ; an' when men an' ministers hae got that intil their heids, it'll help 'em tae mak a better warld than they do noo.

ANDREW. But ye'd hae laws, wadna' ye, Rob-bie ? An' ye'd hae morals ?

BURNS. A wadna' throw in more morals than ye can find keep for in human nature wi'oot scalding it on a fire that maks it boil ower. Ye're telt that manners mak the mon ; but yer ranting morals only mak a muck-heap for mon tae rot.

ANDREW. Ah, Robbie, ye talk as ye wad heed naething !

BURNS. A heed aeverything ! There's no' a bird

flies, nor onything that crawls, A canna tell ye the kind o' it.

ANDREW. Birds havena' souls, mon.

BURNS. Hae they noo'? Then they manage weel wi'oot them : better than we with.

ANDREW. The minister spoke vera powerfully this morning, Robbie.

BURNS. He did—o' the things he kent. But he was powerful foolish ower the ither things.

ANDREW. He frichted me.

BURNS. He meant tae : it's his job. He didna' fricht *me*.

ANDREW. (*Persuasively, wishing his fear to be shared.*) Hell, Robbie !

BURNS. A was thinking o' something better.

ANDREW. Are ye no afraid ye'll go there ?

BURNS. Mon, we're there a'ready—all o' us !

ANDREW. (*With wavering faith.*) An' the Minister ?

BURNS. The Minister's the bottom o' it a'— He's auld Nickie hissel', an' disna ken it.

ANDREW. Robbie ! Ye're blaspheming !

BURNS. Against wha ; . . . Auld Nickie ? . . . Tuh ! Do ony o' us ken wha we really are ? . . . A wish A did. Am A onything but a puir weak mon that happens wad ha' done better no' tae be born ? Onything but a loose crazy loon making rhymes tae tickle the lugs o' the tipplers o' a' the taverns — an' a few lasses, maybe, that had better no' listen tae 'em ? Will A ever be remembered after A'm gone ? What's he that's got haud o' me — here inside ? Is it God, or Deil ? If it's God, why are we always fechting — Him an' me ? If it's the Deil — how is it A hae sich love in me that A'm neebor to whatever has life in it ? The Deil loves naething, except tae torture it. A love æverything. An' oh, mon ! what an agony's the flesh that ye canna' tak the whole warl' in yer arms, an' care for it like as if ye were its ain feyther : fend it frae harm, hush it, warm it, sing tae it till it sleeps! . . . The warld'll end some day. Will there be ony singing in it then ? Will it gae up wi' a merry noise, tae the sound o' the trump ? Eh ! maybe, when a' folk are deid in it, there'll be ae wee lark singing up in the clouds — tae itsel', or tae its mate, maybe ; or just a sparrow chirping on an auld tumbled-in roof where once was a warm hearth, an' a licht, an' the sound o' bairns' voices. . . . Eh, life's hard tae bear, life's hard tae bear, when ye've got much o' it in ye. But A wadna' gie it up — no, no' tae get tae

Heaven—no' yet! That's the truth o' it : we hae got tae be here, an' find oorsel's oot for what we are. But O God, the grief, the trouble o' it! The black doubt whether ye're onything but a speck o' dust picked up oot o' the ground an' blown— blown onywhere till it just falls back again, dust into dust! . . . God! . . .

> (*As he sits silent, the uncomfortable Andy makes a move, but is held when the other breaks out again.*)

Look at me! Look at these hands—a' the movements, an' the strings in them ; an' the shape, an' the strength, an' the knowledge in them o' a' the things they've learned doing, an' loved doing! See the subtlety o' it a' ; an' this tae be only dust! An' that—only a bit o' me! What are they for ? The steering a plough, or the driving o' horses ? the haulding o' a pen ? the handling o' a woman's hair, let doon i' the dark tae cover yer eyes frae the stars ?

ANDREW. Robbie!

BURNS. Or just the putting o' food into yer mouth, or the tipping up o' a pewter-pot ? What are they for, Andy ?

ANDREW. What's onything for ?

BURNS. Yes, that's what A want tae know! What's life for ?

ANDREW. Is't na for living just ? Ye canna get awa frae it.

BURNS. No : nor frae the Deil, either. But ye can get awa frae God, A fear ; an' whar are ye then ?

ANDREW. Ye're preaching the Minister's sermon ower again, Robbie.

BURNS. That blithering, blighted, blind bat ! . . . Am A ? A'd rather be in Hell !

ANDREW. Ye said ye were in it a'ready.

BURNS. Yes ; an' there's more in it o' guid than in a' his preachin'.

ANDREW. Then ye havena repented, A'm thinking.

BURNS. A've repented being born, maybe. But once ye're born, it's hard tae repent the life it brings ye tae. That's it Andy. Ye're *in* life then : there's no going back on it. But ye might wish, as in a dream, that ye never *were* in it. It's the same wi' women, Andy. Till ye ken a woman wi' yer body—or till ye want tae ken her that way—there's peace for a mon. Ye can say that was happiness, looking back. But there's no peace, an' there's no happiness wi' oot her, once ye ken. An' there's no getting oot o' it. It's the same wi' life.

144

Ye may curse yer life ; but ye'll cling tae it tae the bitter end. Aye, an' ye'll gae after it tae the ends o' the earth—if ye'd lost it—tae find it again.

ANDREW. Lost it ? D'ye mean—in the ither warld, Robbie ?

BURNS. A hardly ken what A mean. A said it— as A felt it. Here's life in me—" *my* life," A call it ; but A dinna ken what it is, or what the end o' it a' is tae be. When ye were a bairn, Andy, didna ye feel at times as if something had jumped on tae yer back in the dark, was hauding on, an' wadna' let go ? Ye might twist, ye might turn, but ye couldna get rid o' it. An' ye might run—it liked for ye tae run ; ye might souse yersel' i' the burn— it liked ye tae du that too ; or ye might cast yersel' doon into the pit—and weel it liked for ye to du that ! It 'ud gie ye a' the bogle terrors o' the nicht ; but whatever ye did it telt ye tae du, there was no pleasing the twa o' ye. An' though ye did a' it made ye du, ye'd never be *friends*.

ANDREW. A dinna understaun' what ye mean, mon !

BURNS. No ; ye wadna'. . . . What dae ye say tae this, Andy ? A've begun writing a hymn tae the Deil ; an' surely that ought tae please him weel, dae ye na think sae ? But will it ? . . . Hark, noo !

ANDREW. God forbid ! Ye mauna' pray tae the Deil in a kirk, Robbie !

BURNS. O Thou, whatever title suit thee—
 Auld Hornie, Satan, Nick, or Clootie—
 Wha in yon cavern grim an' sootie,
  Closed under hatches,
 Spairges aboot the brunstane cootie,
  Tae scaud poor wretches !
 Hear me, Auld Hangie, for a wee,
 An' let puir damnèd bodies be ;
 A'm sure sma' pleasure it can gie,
  E'en tae a Deil,
 Tae skelp an' scaud puir dogs like me,
  An' hear us squeal.

What dae ye think o' that for a beginning ?

ANDREW. (*Tremulously.*) A maun go, Robbie.

BURNS. Frichted ye, has it ? Ha !

ANDREW. Surely, mon, A think ye're noo in yer richt senses, talking the way ye've been doing !

BURNS. Who is ? Are ony of oor senses richt ? Can ye trust ane o' 'em ?

ANDREW. A'm going, Robbie.

BURNS. Back hame ? What are ye going tae tell her ?

ANDREW. What dae ye want me tae tell her ?

BURNS. Say, Andy, that A hae had a great time o' it, three hours this morning, wi' the Minister pulling ma lugs, an' her pulling ma hert, an' a' the thrang neebors looking at me. Tell her she's tae be a bra' lass, an' no' tae mind what ony o' them say. Tell her tae kiss the bairn for me, an' gie tae't its feyther's love. Tell her A'll come roun' an' see her when they let me; or if they wilna', A'll come ma ain gait by stealth after dark. She'll like that better, maybe. An', Andy, tell her A've made a rhyme a' aboot her an' me, that'll be remembered an' sung lang after she an' A are gone tae heaven thegither.

> (*Andrew, meanwhile, with apprehensive look, has been fingering the latch, impatient to be off. Seeing this, the other checks the flow of his discourse, and curtly dismisses him.*)

There! Ye can gae. Aff wi' ye – quick!

> (*Much relieved, Andrew slips out.*)

BURNS. Eh! What a puir fool Andy is—what a puir, weak fool! . . . Oh, this warld, this warld; an' we are in it! Oh, God, God! How can A stick it oot? How can A bear it? Life! An' A still sae young! An' if, after a', A do that which shall make the warld remember me – what then? What's the guid of it?

147

(*With a sudden freeing of the emotions, pitiful and childlike, he falls on his knees, and bowing over the cutty-stool prays as from the depth of his heart. Perhaps the words being in verse are a help to him, so making them seem more his own; but anyway, for the time being, here is sincere and utter surrender.*)

O Lord, oot o' the deeps o' Hell,
  It is tae Thee I cry:
Oh, let Thine ear consider well
  This voice o' misery!

If Thou, O Lord, art strict tae sum
  What man has done amiss,
Tae whom, then, shall salvation come?
  What hope for sin is this?

Ma feet are stuck in mire an' clay,
  Ma mind is hedged with doot,
Sae bound in prison A am, A pray;
  But naething brings me oot!

(*Above his head a door opens; from the way by which he went out, the Minister returns, now divested of his gown. He advances, and stands looking down on the bowed penitent, who, becoming aware of him, stiffens and slowly raises himself.*)

148

MINISTER.　Sae the Lord has searched thee oot, an' has shown thee thy sin !

> (*Burns rises ; the cutty-stool clutched in his hand, he stands erect.*)

BURNS.　Aye ; there's a fine repentance for ye, noo at last ! — till next time ; thanks tae yer sermon, Minister.　Ye did richt tae get spew-quit o' it when ye did !　It's the kind that winna' keep !

> (*Flinging the cutty-stool violently down, so that it breaks, he turns and goes quickly out by the door behind him.*)

MINISTER.　Ah !　There's a sair example o' a hard hert !　A fear there'll be no mending him.

> (*Blithely, from without, comes the sound of a voice calling "Andy." The door swings to with a slam. The Minister picks up the cutty-stool, to restore it to its legs ; one of them he finds broken. On that he makes up his mind — and speaks it.*)

Twal' bawbees that shall cost him — twal' bawbees, or a summons !

Elegy of a Country Churchyard

Characters

THOMAS GRAY.

THE SEXTON.

A GRAVE-DIGGER.

SOME GENTRY.

SOME VILLAGERS.

THE RECTOR.

THOMAS GRAY
From a painting by J. G. Eccardt (National Portrait Gallery)

Elegy of a Country Churchyard

October, 1742.

*The churchyard of Stoke Poges is looking quite uncon-
scious of itself : for though the curfew is tolling,
while lowing herd and ploughman occupy their
classic places in the landscape, the Elegy has not
yet been written. But it is being written. The
poet Gray sits on a tomb under the church wall,
note-book in hand ; and though his eye is not
rolling in the fine frenzy which poetry is supposed
to demand, his tongue is murmuring poetic phrases
which are destined to become immortal. But it is
all being done (as, in the eighteenth century, it
always was) in a quiet and gentlemanly fashion ;
and you might pass along the churchyard path to
the gate (as the sexton presently does, when his
bell-ringing is over), and think that the gentleman
was only doing up his accounts, or copying down
an epitaph ; for — as a later poet said of him —
Thomas Gray " never spoke out " ; modest, re-
served, retiring, he was at all times pre-eminently
well-conducted ; and though, in the course of his*

life things often shocked and disturbed him, he himself shocked and disturbed nobody. And his poetry was like himself: no immortal poem has ever taken its place in the language in a more quiet and sedentary fashion than the famous Elegy; like "Abide with Me!" it seems always to have been there; the sequence of English poetry would be incomplete without it; and it remains to this day the poem which, in proportion to its length, contains the greatest number of phrases that have passed into current use.

Mr. Gray is wearing an overcoat; and that is as well, for now, after sunset, the air has turned chilly, and gradually from the ground there rises (or seems to rise) a mist that grows dense, obscuring the crowded gravestones which jostle for place— humble satellites of the big railed tomb which stands toward the centre. From behind it earth-clods are being thrown to the surface by an invisible hand—indication that down below a grave is preparing for to-morrow's use, and must be finished before nightfall. A touch so topical should surely have helped the composition; but in his opening stanzas Mr. Gray has not mentioned it; only the bell claims his attention; and to its accompanying verberations he first utters audibly, then writes down, poetic lines in a form less perfect and polished than that which the world now knows.

GRAY. The curfew sounds the knell of passing day . . . " sounds ? "—no : " tolls " . . . " passing " . . . " passing " . . . ah ! " parting ! " That's better ! . . . That makes a good opening, at any rate ! (*Thereupon he recites the amended version before entering it in his note-book.*)

> The curfew tolls the knell of parting day,
> > The lowing herd into the distance goes,
> The ploughman homeward plods his weary
> > way,
> > And leaves the world to darkness and
> > repose.

" Goes " . . . " repose " : now is that quite . . . I wonder ? Or better shall I say " to me "? and then " lea " would rhyme with it.

> (*He is pondering the point still undecided, when—the bell having ceased to ring— the sexton comes out and locks the door. It is unusual at this hour to find anyone in the churchyard. The poet sits abstracted ; the old man, slow of mind, stands and looks at him.*)

SEXTON. Was you waiting for the Rector, sir ? He's dining at Squire's, and won't be back for an hour.

GRAY. (*Patiently irritated.*) No, no . . . *no.* I'm not waiting for anyone !

(*From a distance comes a clatter of hoofs and the sound of a bugle. This rouses the sexton's interest, but not the poet's.*)

SEXTON. Ah! There be the troops, going back to Windsor. . . . Good night, sir.

(*He has turned and gone down to the gate before Gray comes out of his reveries sufficiently to answer :*)

GRAY. Good night. . . . Now, why, why, why did he interrupt me ? So unnecessary ; so disturbing !

(*He is settling to his writing again, when there comes another interruption : the church clock striking the hour ; the chimes follow. They play — a little out of key — Luther's well-known " judgment hymn " : the tune is an ill-chosen one, for, as it ranges into the bass beyond the octave, it requires adaptation, and the note which should be the lowest lifts, and with perky interrogation becomes the highest : the sort of thing which constantly happens in churches whose chimes have only eight bells. Mr. Gray, however, is not musical : he is only bored. He lays down his note-book, and with a sigh of resignation, leaning his head*)

156

against the church wall, waits for the interruption to end. As the tune repeats itself for the third and last time, a voice rises from the earth. The gravedigger, having finished his job, turns to religion; and as he does so, once more the bugle is blown. Coming up from the ground he fits words to tune, and as the chimes reach their concluding phrase—sings with them, through the nose, rather dolefully :)

GRAVEDIGGER. "The trumpet sounds, the graves restore
The dead which they contained before.
Prepare, my soul, to meet Him!"

Aye : but there's a many of 'em there as *won't* be prepared . . . want to stick their 'eads in the ground, they will *then*. Eh, eh, eh!

(To this composer of corpses the thought is not unpleasing ; and off he goes with dry uncharitable chucklings over the uncomfortable end awaiting the many he has known. And now all interruptions are over ; but perhaps from the fact that he has dined well—these being the days of the four o'clock dinner—the Poet continues to recline in an attitude more sug-

157

gestive of repose than meditation : has, in fact, gone to sleep. That, to say the least of it, is a pity ; for something is now taking place in the churchyard, more exciting even than the composition of a famous poem : Under the closing-in of night, and the rising of ground-mist, the graves are opening ; and slowly, deliberately, and a little doubtfully, people are coming out of them. Be they bodies or be they ghosts, their rising seems to bring moonlight, and moonlight of an extra special quality : vivid and unearthly, it fills the churchyard with a cold steely radiance, and the shadows cast by it are not black and opaque, like those to which night accustoms us, but blue, luminous, and opalescent. If the figures were as beautiful as the atmosphere it might almost be a scene from fairyland : but they are not. In all their lineaments and characteristics, they are of the earth earthy, very rustic, most of them old, slow, and stiff of movement, as though still crippled by the infirmities of which they died ; and when they speak, there is nothing heavenward or elevating in their mode of utterance.)

1st RUSTIC. Wull! wull! wull! What be all this about? Seems to me I be light-'eaded.

2nd RUSTIC. Seems to me we all be.

3rd RUSTIC. Where do we be coming from?

2nd RUSTIC. From our graves, it do look like.

1st RUSTIC. Our graves? What took us there? How did we get into them?

4th RUSTIC. There's only one way a man gets into his grave—by dying.

3rd RUSTIC. Dying? I ain't dead!

4th RUSTIC. You was, though—minute ago. Aye! We'm all been dead and buried. Now we'm risen again—means Judgment's come, I reckon.

3rd RUSTIC. Judgment? You call this Judgment?

4th RUSTIC. Seems like we'm waiting for it— seeing they've got us *out*.

2nd RUSTIC. *Who's* got us out?

4th RUSTIC. I wouldn't take on me for to say. But we 'aven't done it ourselves.

1st RUSTIC. Dead, and buried, and now risen again? Then where's all the rest on us?

4th RUSTIC. If they 'aven't come up—maybe

they'm gone *down*. There's *some*'ll 'ave to, we know.

3rd RUSTIC. No ; look 'ee there ! There's his worship the Squire coming up. If he do come *up*, I reckon nobody goes *down !*

1st RUSTIC. Aye : and he's got his lady with 'im too. Ho ! (*This seems to give them amusement.*)

2nd RUSTIC. And there's other of the quality, look ! coming up yonder ! There's old Parson !

> (*The pair to which their attention has been specially directed are the occupants of the central tomb, which stands within its own grounds, so to speak, behind railings. Manners, as well as dress, still mark the distinction of their rank as they step up into future life. The Squire hands forward his lady with the same respect that he has always shown to her in public ; but the railings are a barrier : there is however a gap through which the lady, who is slim, now tries to pass.*)

SQUIRE. Where *are* you going, my dear ?

LADY. I'm sure I don't know where *either* of us is going, Sir James ! That is no longer for *us* to decide.

SQUIRE. Then hadn't we better wait till

Heaven — that is, wait for the key, and get out in the proper way ?

LADY. I hope it *will* be the proper way, for *both* of us. But you didn't always lead a good life, Sir James. After you died, *I found things out !*

SQUIRE. (*Quite unabashed.*) You did, did you ? Which of 'em ?

LADY. All of them, I *hope.*

SQUIRE. Not at all likely, my dear.

LADY. And I've wondered since whether poor Richard's being killed, and leaving you without an heir, wasn't God's judgment on you for it.

SQUIRE. " Judgment " ? You know it was only an accident. And had you done your duty and had more children, it wouldn't have mattered.

LADY. (*Tartly.*) So *you* made up for it — elsewhere.

SQUIRE. I did, and I'm not ashamed of it !

LADY. Well, I hope to-day you'll be able to know them again.

SQUIRE. Aye : a wise father, they say, should——

(*He breaks off ; for at that moment, very conveniently, the Parson, who has risen*

L   161

*from an adjoining grave, advances to
pay his respects.*)

Ah, Parson! Glad to see you again. How are
you? Well?

PARSON. Indeed, Sir James, under the circumstances, better than I could have expected. I hope
I see your ladyship well?

SQUIRE. Parson, where is the key? We want to
get out.

PARSON. The sexton has the key, Sir James. No
doubt he has gone for it.

LADY. Oh, la! What's coming to me? I feel
quite giddy!

SQUIRE. Sit down, my dear, sit down!

LADY. (*Seating herself.*) The tombs all open :
everything so different!

PARSON. Yes, indeed! And so many of my own
burying. Very disturbing : but of course what one
was always told *would* happen.

> (*And now others of the quality come forward
> to exchange greetings. Meanwhile two
> rustics, who have stooped to inspect an
> open grave, are in colloquy with its
> occupant.*)

162

1st RUSTIC. Ain't you coming up, Timothy ?

TIMOTHY. (*From below.*) What should I come up for ?

2nd RUSTIC. Everyone else 'as come up, pretty nigh.

TIMOTHY. Who made 'em ?

2nd RUSTIC. You don't need much making when the grave opens for you.

TIMOTHY. Fools don't ! I'm comfortable where I am ; stay here till I'm fetched.

1st RUSTIC. But that's not scriptural, Timothy. The dead's got to rise when they'm told.

TIMOTHY. Nobody 'aven't told *me*. Parson up ?

1st RUSTIC. Aye, over there, paying his respects to Squire and Squire's lady.

TIMOTHY. Jim Hampden up ?

2nd RUSTIC. I ain't seen him : but his grave's open.

TIMOTHY. So's mine. Let 'im lie ! There'll be trouble between 'im and Squire, if 'e comes up.

1st RUSTIC. That right o' way, ye mean ?

TIMOTHY. Ah, where's that gone now ? (*Chuckles.*)

163

2nd RUSTIC. I wonder ye don't come up to see what world be like, Timothy.

TIMOTHY. I know what the world's like. I seed 'n for sixty years and more.

2nd RUSTIC. Eh, but now it's different.

TIMOTHY. Don't want to see it, then.

3rd RUSTIC. (*Joining them.*) Church be the same.

1st RUSTIC. Aye : church 'aven't changed.

3rd RUSTIC. And churchyard's the same.

2nd RUSTIC. More graves, though.

3rd RUSTIC. And fewer in 'em.

1st RUSTIC. Aye : Timothy's doing the honours for all of us now. D'you think they'll let you stay there, Timothy ?

TIMOTHY. I'll stay till they don't.

2nd RUSTIC. Oh ! hark, yon ! 'S a hell of a row going on over there !

1st RUSTIC. What's about ?

2nd RUSTIC. Jim Hampden's found his right o' way gone. (*Laughs maliciously.*)

TIMOTHY. (*Emerging.*) Hampden up ? What ha' they told 'im ?

2nd RUSTIC. (*Pointing.*) That yonder there's stables across it, and a wall.

TIMOTHY. (*With relish.*) Oh! What'll he say to that?

1st RUSTIC. He's saying it now!

> (*And at this moment the village Hampden is to be seen pushing his way through a crowd of his fellows, one of whom speaks soothingly but in vain.*)

HAMPDEN. I'll see 'em damned first!

4th RUSTIC. Well, it lasted *your* time. What's the matter with you?

HAMPDEN. Nobody hadn't the right to touch it.

3rd RUSTIC. Somebody has the right to do anything.

HAMPDEN. No, they haven't : not to a right of way, they haven't!

3rd RUSTIC. Act of Parliament can do it.

HAMPDEN. *Bribery* can do it—when there's no *man* to stand against it. Eh, you were all sheep— all of you!

4th RUSTIC. And a mad dog *you* were! See what's come of it!

HAMPDEN. Well, if this be Judgment Day, let's have judgment, and the fellow damned as did it!

TIMOTHY. Eh, you got your job cut out, then! Squire did it!

HAMPDEN. Squire!

PARSON. (*Intervening.*) Now, my man, this won't do at all. Remember you are in a churchyard.

HAMPDEN. And wasn't our right of way through churchyard? Wasn't it here? Where is it now— with his fine tomb sticking up in the middle of it?

SQUIRE. Yes, you low fellow, where is it? Gone : like everything else *you* stood for.

HAMPDEN. I'll have the law on you!

SQUIRE. Too late ; law of limitations. You've been dead too long. It's *my* right of way now.

HAMPDEN. Not if this be the Day of Judgment, it shan't be!

SQUIRE. And who is the judge of that, pray?

HAMPDEN. If God doesn't—I will! *We* will!

1st RUSTIC. Ah! but you can't do that to Squire ; not against Squire you can't do it!

HAMPDEN. I'd do it against the King himself.

SQUIRE. You say that before a magistrate ? Here, Sexton ! Where is that key ? Open ! I must get out.

SEXTON. Key be here, Squire ; but key ain't no use ; lock's rusty — broke.

SQUIRE. But I must get out of this somehow.

HAMPDEN. (*Challengingly.*) Why ?

PARSON. Couldn't you perhaps climb over, Sir James ?

(*He tries, but very soon desists.*)

HAMPDEN. (*Derisively.*) Get a ladder sent down to you from Heaven, as you think you are going there !

SQUIRE. Ha ! Insolent fellow !

> (*He makes for the gap in the railings and, giving his hat to the Parson to hold, tries to get through. After a long attempt he sticks there. Meanwhile from the sleeping Poet comes a murmur of speech :*)

GRAY. Some Village Hampden, that with daunt-
less breast
Withstood the petty tyrant of his
fields.

> (*Passing by, the Village Poet turns and looks at him.*)

VILLAGE POET. What was that you said ? That sounded like poetry. I write poetry too.

(*But the sleeping Poet pays no attention. Another, who has just been contemplating his own tomb, does so, however.*)

TOMB-OWNER. You write stuff that you *call* poetry ; and you put it on men's grave-stones when they can't help themselves. See here what you put on mine ! What d'you mean by it ?

VILLAGE POET. Whatever you want it to mean, friend. I leave that to you.

TOMB-OWNER. (*Reading.*) " Reader, pass by !
                Stay not to waste your time
On most indifferent prose, on much worse rhyme :
What I was once this stone and grave manures "—

VILLAGE POET. (*Correctively.*) Immures.

TOMB-OWNER. " What I am now is no concern
                of yours."
What you write that about *me* for ?

VILLAGE POET. Isn't it quite true — true of anybody who's dead ?

TOMB-OWNER. Not so long as you've a tombstone over you. You're everybody's concern then : else what be a stone for ?

VILLAGE POET. Mainly to keep others out, I should say. I know no better reason.

TOMB-OWNER. Where's your own ? What did you have put on that ?

VILLAGE POET. Only the sad truth.

TOMB-OWNER. Let's have it !

VILLAGE POET. (*Reciting.*) A mute inglorious Milton here I lie,
My name and years, spelt by th' unlettered Muse,
The place of fame and elegy supply.
When hope lies withered, oh, the rest excuse !

LADY. (*Encouragingly.*) And very pretty, I'm sure !

VILLAGE POET. Thank you, my lady !

GRAY. (*Again composing in his sleep.*) Some mute inglorious Milton here may rest : Some——

VILLAGE POET. (*Eager for appreciation.*) Yes ; "mute inglorious": a good phrase isn't it ? I was rather struck by that myself.

LADY. Sir James, when are we going to get out ? I don't call *that* the proper way !

SQUIRE. (*Angrily.*) Well, I'm not stuck here for my own pleasure, woman !

(*Pauper's ground has now given up its insig-*

169

*nificant dead. As though still knowing
their place, they have remained unobtru-
sively in the background ; but one of a
more pushing character now comes forward and speaks :)*

PAUPER. No ; now it be for *ours !* Aye ; you
was the one as used to put me in the stocks. Who's
in the stocks now ?

PARSON. (*Correctively.*) Please to remember
that you are in a churchyard !

PAUPER. Well, that levels us anyway — first
time ! We be all alike now Judgment's come.

2nd RUSTIC. But it *haven't* come. Where is it ?
We be all waiting.

LADY. Sir James, if you can't get through, I
think you'd better come back. You are making an
exhibition of yourself.

PARSON. Yes, do, Sir James. If your ladyship
will give a pull while I give a push. . . .

(*They do so, and succeed.*)

SQUIRE. Ah, that's better !

2nd RUSTIC. Yes, as I say : 'ere we *hall hare* — and
must be judged by somebody. Heaven don't
seem to be in no hurry to do it herself ; but we
must 'ave a judge somehow.

SQUIRE. (*Consequentially*.) Ah, H'm! H'm!

HAMPDEN. Ho? Got that off your fat belly, have you?

SQUIRE. A judge you said, eh? Well, I presume that, even in the next world, I am still a Justice of the Peace.

> (*But meantime the Village Hampden has not been idle ; by dint of threats, argument and pressure, he has secured followers, and with these he now declares himself.*)

HAMPDEN. Justice of the Peace? This ain't no piece-work ; this is for the whole damn lot of us — *you*, too! Ho! We ain't going to be judged by *you*, God-Squire! No fear!

PAUPER. You done that for us in life. Now's come the day that puts down the mighty from their seats what has assaulted the humble and meek. It's the humble and meek, Squire, that's going to sit in judgment here. It's the turn of the worm now! Eh, neighbours, what do you say?

TIMOTHY. Eh! powerful spoke, lad! But I don't 'ave no hand in it. If I went after doing 'Eaven's job for 'er, 'Eaven might come after *me*.

(*Enter Beadle from grave at the rear.*)

HAMPDEN. Let 'er come! And for once she'll find justice being done. Prisoner!

RUSTIC. Why, look ! here be Beadle coming ! Beadle, you be late !

PARSON. Quick, quick Beadle ! You are wanted.

SQUIRE. Beadle ! Put that fellow in the stocks !

BEADLE. (*Timorously.*) Please, your worship, I——

> (*His foot slips on the edge of a grave : he disappears.*)

HAMPDEN. It's no use, Squire, *you* are in the dock now. Here, call the jury !

> (*While he continues speaking, twelve good men and true are selected and stand ranged.*)

When you put up those rails, you didn't think what they'd come to be used for, did you ? They was put for to keep out we common folk. Now it's you, *un*common folk, they be there to keep in.

> (*The Beadle has now re-emerged, and has ranged himself cautiously on the side of the stronger numbers.*)

Beadle, if the prisoner don't conduct himself as a prisoner should, you teach him ! If you don't, we'll teach you !

PARSON. Really, all this is very irregular !

HAMPDEN. Would you like to go into the dock,

172

too, Parson ? You can if you like ! 'Twas you let him take our right of way from us.

PARSON. I was quite powerless in the matter.

HAMPDEN. Then you've got to keep powerless now ! Now then — there's the prisoner at the bar ; where are the witnesses ?

SQUIRE. Witnesses — to what pray ? What charge have you against me ?

HAMPDEN. We charge you with being a bad character, Squire ; and a bad judge of the characters of others ; men and women alike you been bad to. Nor we won't call your own wife a witness against you either. There's plenty more to speak to it.

LADY. My husband's character is *his* concern and mine, and no one's else. Such impudence as yours deserves a whipping !

HAMPDEN. Spoke like a good wife ! You can come out of the dock if you like, lady.

STRANGER. (*Pushing his way forward.*) No one's else ? No one's else ? What about *me* ?

(*All turn to look ; but he stands unrecognised.*)

SQUIRE. Well, what about you ? Who are you ?

STRANGER. Reuben Grain's my name.

(*The Squire starts and grows agitated.*)

Committed for trial by *you*, I was transported for life for what your son done — killing a keeper " *by accident*."

SQUIRE. Transported for life ? Then how did you get back ?

REUBEN. How I got back doesn't matter. When I got back there was none left to know me ; twelve years out there changes a man. (*To Squire's lady*.) So *his* character's not *my* concern, eh ?

SQUIRE. I but committed you for trial. You were tried by your own countrymen. I did not *know* that you were innocent.

REUBEN. Not then. . . . But you did afterwards. You were given *proof*. . . . Did you speak ?

SQUIRE. *I* had not judged you.

REUBEN. No ; only committed me — sent me for trial. And when you *knew* — had proof — did you commit your son ? Did you send *him* for trial ?

SQUIRE. My son died — by an accident.

REUBEN. Twelve years after, that was. "Accident " ? No : *I'd* come back ; and 'twas no *accident*.

*(My lady's hand goes to her heart; the
Squire, rising, bends forward, gripping
the rails of his tomb.)*

Yes. Here's come Day of Judgment. And the
thing I'm proudest of before God — the one thing
I did in all those twelve years that made life worth
living was — *when I killed your son* — " *by accident* " !

LADY. Oh, God !

PARSON. Madam, calm yourself !

PAUPER. Got him ! Got him ! In under the
fifth rib !

REUBEN. *(Vengefully.)* Your only son !

SQUIRE. *(Pulling himself together with a certain
dignity.)* No ; not my *only* son. Hear me ! When
I did that, I but sacrificed one of my sons to save
another.

*(My lady collapses weeping. There is a long
pause. Then Reuben turns, walks slowly
away, and disappears. They turn and
stare after him.)*

1st RUSTIC. Who'd 'a thought it ! Who'd ever
'a thought that ?

TIMOTHY. Ah ! *I* knew.

175

HAMPDEN. Any other witness ?

(*A woman comes forward.*)

WOMAN. I could 'a said summat ; but I won't now.

HAMPDEN. Any other ?

POACHER. Do you know *me*, Squire ?

SQUIRE. Yes : you are the rascal that fought me over that bit of land.

POACHER. Yes, and beat you over it, too. And got beaten for it—beaten to death by your keepers. Was anyone hanged for *that ?*

SQUIRE. We don't hang men who kill poachers.

POACHER. I was no poacher, *then !* 'Twas on my own land ; and they carried me on to yours, so as to make it seem . . . I was another of your sons, Squire, but that *you* didn't know.

HAMPDEN. Any other ?

WOMAN. Which other ? There's many, but there's no need now.

HAMPDEN. You be judged, Squire !

> (*But,* as the word is said, attention is di-
> verted ; for once again the Poet stirs in
> his sleep, and speaks :)

GRAY. No farther seek his merits to disclose,
The struggling pangs of conscious truth to hide ;
Nor draw his frailties from their dead repose
Within yon shrine of Luxury and Pride.

Can storied urn, or animated bust
Back to its mansion call the fleeting breath ?
Can Honour's voice provoke——

> (*And while his voice drones on, something is
> happening ; a curious spirit of irresolu-
> tion takes hold of the assembled crowd ;
> attention wavers ; the mist thickens, the
> moonlight begins to fail ; the forms grow
> vague and are drifting away. One of
> the Rustics turns, and stooping down
> looks at the sleeping Poet. Across the
> crooned words his voice breaks in.*)

RUSTIC. Who be here ? Why don't *he* wake
too ? Still dead, eh ?

VILLAGE POET. (*With a higher sense of the truth.*)
No ; he's not dead—never was—is still alive. He's
only sleeping.

> (*He looks earnestly into the sleeper's face.
> Then turns and speaks with a kind of
> authority.*)

And this is no Day of Judgment : we are not risen.
We are only his dream !

RUSTIC. (*Annoyed, giving Gray a sharp kick.*) His *dream* ? Then let him wake !

(*And as Gray does so, the dream disperses in mist. The forms all disappear ; the graves close again.*)

GRAY. (*Rubbing first his eyes, then his kicked shin.*) Oh ! but this is most distressing ! Rheumatism, I'm afraid ! Asleep ? Oh, why was I so careless ?

(*And just then, along the churchyard path, comes the Rector.*)

RECTOR. (*Chidingly.*) Mr. Gray ! Mr. Gray ! Mr. Gray ! Sitting on a cold, damp stone, after sunset, and in a churchyard too !

GRAY. I'm afraid I was *asleep* on it — very careless of me !

RECTOR. (*Astonished.*) You have been asleep *here* ?

GRAY. I *have* been asleep here, and unfortunately have had a dream.

RECTOR. Why unfortunately ? Surely a dream doesn't matter.

GRAY. Indeed it does — in this instance.

RECTOR. But, pray, why ?

GRAY. I was writing a poem, sir; a poem by which I hoped to become famous. Writing the poem, I fell asleep, and dreamed. And unfortunately the dream and the poem do not harmonise.

RECTOR. Well, even so, the dream has gone; the poem remains.

GRAY. No; the dream remains also. And until I forget the dream, I shall never finish the poem!

RECTOR. Then forget it, sir!

GRAY. I wish I could. No; it will take me years now to finish my poem.

RECTOR. Dear, dear, dear! You don't say so! What a dreadful fate!

GRAY. Yes; to have to think of nothing else for years!—just think—how tired of it I shall get!

RECTOR. And when you've done it, how tired of it everyone *else* will get!

GRAY. (*Despondently.*) Perhaps so. . . . I daresay!

RECTOR. Drop it, my dear sir!

GRAY. I almost think I will!

RECTOR. Yes, drop it! Take my advice, and write another. You know the wise saying, " There

are as good fish in the sea as ever came out of it ":
the same is true with poems. You put one aside,
another takes its place. What else is the imagination for, if not to find change of subject ?

GRAY. But this was such a good subject.

RECTOR. Oh, you'll find a better ! You'll find
a better ! Now go home, and take a little something warming to the stomach ! Good night !

GRAY. (*Despondently.*) Good night !

(*And once more he is alone.*)

Yes ; if I can only both remember *and* forget.

(*His memory starts on the desired selection.*)

Hampden, " some Village Hampden . . . some
mute inglorious Milton " . . . just *that* . . . and
let all the rest go. Oh, but now it is going to take
me at least nine years !

(*And it did !*)

Sal Volatile

Characters

NINON DE LANCLOS
> (*A Lady with a Reputation*).

NANNETTE
> (*Her Maid*).

JEAN CLAUDE
> (*An unwelcome Intruder*).

CHARLES DE SEVIGNÉ
> (*An accepted Lover*).

NINON DE LANCLOS
From a painting by P. Mignart (Musées Royaux des Beaux Arts de Belgique)

Sal Volatile

A DIALOGUE OF DOUBTFUL VIRTUE.

1670.

The small square chamber with its embrasured window, in the rue des Tournelles, shows the perfect taste of its occupant. Mounting from that quiet narrow street of the Paris of the seventeenth century, one enters what in effect might almost be a Temple, or at least its ante-chamber. Everything here is so designed, or so disposed, that it has the air of attendance upon rites only temporarily in abeyance. Upon either side of a curtained doorway to an inner chamber stand two candelabra, their candles at the present moment unlighted, but crowned nevertheless with imitation flames of gilded wax. The painted coffer, placed at a slight remove, guarding but not obstructing the door of the inner sanctum, has all the conscious repose of an altar accustomed to service. Upon its napery of fine lace stands a casket, containing, one ventures

183

*to suppose, precious ointments not destined for the
poor. The dove with outspread wings filling the
central tracery of the window may be a little less
holy than its form suggests, for the small polished
vessel of bright enamel with its silver chain, lying
open upon the table below, is not a thurible but a
pomander. Its owner, a lady of ripe but youthful
appearance, beneath which fifty unbelievable
years lie concealed, sits delicately released from
the stiff fashions of her day in a rose-tinted robe,
loose but respectful in its embrace. From beneath
its hem peeps a gilded slipper ; and over her dark
hair a fabric of gold tissue whispers the fact that
the hour for full toilette has not yet arrived. She
has been reading a book which she lays gently
aside, when her maid, looking a little frightened,
enters, and stands hesitant at the door.*

NINON. Well, Nannette ; who is it ?

NANNETTE. Monsieur the Philosopher, Madame.
I cannot bring to myself his name.

NINON. Tell Monsieur the Philosopher to
bring it himself.

> *(Nannette retires ; and Ninon sits medita-
> tively fingering her book, waiting the
> Philosopher's arrival. Presently, with a
> slight exclamation of surprise, she sees
> enter not a Doctor of Science, but a*

184

Doctor of Divinity, though, in Paris at all events, the divinity of Monsieur Jean Claude is not legally recognised, and the degree which his dress indicates must have come from Geneva.

Each shows a consciousness, in the first moment of encounter, that a liberty has been taken ; and indeed the establishment of so professional a lady as Ninon de Lanclos has a more assured position in the Catholic France of 1670 than the discountenanced ministry of even so distinguished a theologian and evangelist as Monsieur Jean Claude. But the awkwardness is soon over : Madame has her manners, and the Minister his mission—both products of a training which has become second nature. The saint bows respectfully to the sinner ; and it is the sinner who has first word.)

NINON. What ? Again, Monsieur ?

CLAUDE. Again, Madame. God's controversy with the human soul never ends till death.

NINON. You effected your entry by subterfuge, Monsieur. Is that His method, or only yours ?

CLAUDE. I have come at the call of duty. My office gives me no choice.

185

NINON. By bribing my servant.

CLAUDE. But indeed no, Madame !

NINON. But indeed yes, Monsieur ! Conscience can be bribed to virtue as well as to other things, and not by money only. Simple, and superstitious, conscientiously she has once more admitted you.

CLAUDE. Without any promise of reward, Madame. That I assure you.

NINON. Except in a future life. You were not so negligent, I trust, as to omit that element of temptation ?

CLAUDE. If I could tempt you, Madame, in the same direction, this intrusion would then be forgiven me.

NINON. You may try, Monsieur. But am I equally free to tempt you — in *my* direction ?

CLAUDE. Madame permits herself a pleasantry which I must not resent.

NINON. In my own house, many, Monsieur. Temptation finds itself more at home here, than does repentance.

CLAUDE. Alas, I can well believe it. And it is for that reason that I come again.

NINON. Believing yourself immune, Monsieur — or only inoculated ?

186

CLAUDE. God helping me, Madame, I have no fear of what flesh can do unto me.

NINON. God helps all of us, Monsieur, to lead the life which seems best to us, and to avoid that which we have no use for. But to-day, it would seem, He has been inattentive. For to speak truly, Monsieur, as you have no use for me, neither have I use for you.

CLAUDE. I bow, Madame, to the reproof. I do not deny that the position in which, coming here, I have placed myself is not an easy one.

NINON. I beg then, Monsieur, that you will be seated.

CLAUDE. Ah, no, Madame—I would not presume to seem so familiar. Here I am only your servant, being also my Master's. It is not with one whose favours so many seek, in admiration and flattery and devotion, that I crave permission to speak now. I come to plead, with all the urgency at my command, with pity also and with holy fear, for the soul of one who is a great sinner.

NINON. But what can be more familiar than that, Monsieur? For that, surely, it is not sufficient that you should sit down. Kneel, prostrate yourself! There are cushions and a carpet which you will find accommodating. Nay, do not

187

hesitate, Monsieur ; it is an attitude which I am well accustomed to see men as brave as yourself indulge in, when I am as reluctant to their plea as you will find me to yours.

CLAUDE. Unhappy woman ! Is it so, without shame, that you still mock at me ?

NINON. Of course, Monsieur. On such an errand, what else can you expect ? If I am as evil as you are forced to think me, and if you are as virtuous in your intentions as you profess, what can you expect but mockery ? In your religion mockery has played a part which you must recognise. By that the saints proved themselves — they were above mockery. Be a saint, Monsieur !

CLAUDE. For God's sake I implore you, Madame, to listen to me.

NINON. Do not implore, Monsieur, or compromise your virtue by any words short of the truth ! Command, denounce, speak with the authority you claim. Since you have come self-invited, rid yourself entirely of any manners you have. If you can find language to bring back to my face the blush of shame which it has forgotten, use it, I beg of you ! I recognise that to be a sincere professor of the Reformed Faith, so comparatively new to its task, makes correct conduct difficult. You have not that tradition to help you which Catholics possess. And even they did not come by it till after a long training ; for it is only in this enlightened age, and perhaps only in France, that they have learned to treat the Devil politely.

CLAUDE. Tradition did not exist among the first Christians, Madame ; yet they subdued kings and conquered nations.

NINON. The early Christians, Monsieur, were no gentlemen. They were the nouveaux riches of the spiritual world ; and it was very largely for their bad manners that they were put to death. Your national Synod in its controversies with the Church fell into a like error and has suffered accordingly. And since you, Monsieur, belong to that body which officially says " harlot " to the Catholic Church, be official to me also. It will not be good manners ; but it will prove both your consistency and your sincerity—things which, for their rarity, one should value.

CLAUDE. Were I to bandy words with you, Madame, my use here would be wasted. O frail weak vessel of sin ! where, when you die, do you think to find yourself ?

NINON. That is a question, Monsieur, which all the religions of the world have answered differently. And as I belong to none of them, I do not profess to have an answer. I am content to await the denouement.

CLAUDE. Where will be the contentment, when before your eyes the pit opens its mouth ? Then will it be too late.

NINON. Indeed no, Monsieur ; I have no reason to think so. When I come into the next world I shall knock ; and if I discover there is a God at home in it, on my faith as a lady, I believe I shall find that He is a gentleman.

CLAUDE. You use language, Madame——

NINON. Of the world I know, Monsieur. You have come to use language to me of a world you do not really know, but accept on faith—a faith which I do not share, but which you seek to impose on me.

CLAUDE. The history of the world has proved it to be true. In no other light does the story of man stand credible. Denying that faith, you impose upon yourself. You shut your eyes wilfully : you remain blind till blindness becomes your portion for ever.

NINON. But the blind, Monsieur, do not shut their eyes wilfully. Blindness is an infirmity which deserves pity.

CLAUDE. The blindness of the soul is no infirmity. It is an act of man's will, which deserves damnation.

NINON. But divine justice should not be evaded, Monsieur. Why seek to escape our deserts? And how, in any case?

CLAUDE. Grace, — grace alone can save you.

NINON. Grace? It is a word I know well; but you must mean something different; something I have not yet experienced. If the sinner is to find grace in a new form, first it must attract him. How are you going to attract me?

CLAUDE. Surely by the cloud of witness that you see around you. Are not the feet of the messengers, — are not the lives of the saints lovely to behold?

NINON. Catholic or Protestant, Monsieur? I cannot admire both, when their mission seems to be to kill each other. No wonder I prefer, from such grace, to stand aside.

CLAUDE. Ah! you pretend that you have no chosen religion; but it is still the old superstition which is blinding you. Humble yourself to penitence, that the true light of the Gospel may shine on you. From that darkness in which you now are, you confess that you know nothing of what lies ahead. Have you no fear where the course you follow is leading you ?

NINON. None, Monsieur. No more than the fresh-water stream fears the ocean, however salt to the taste. Finding myself between banks, I follow them.

CLAUDE. Do you believe you were placed in the world for no reason but to enjoy yourself ?

NINON. Whatever placed me in the world, Monsieur, and for whatever reason,—must have placed things in me for a like reason. We have each a little world of our own, full of curious lives all wanting to live and fulfil themselves. Is there not sufficient reason that I, as benefactress to my own world, should say " yes " to them rather than " no " ? But " reason," Monsieur, " reason " ? Why talk of reason ? For my part I live rather by faith, and by instinct.

CLAUDE. But faith and instinct are not the same ; they cannot be,—they are utterly opposed —as light is to darkness.

NINON. Look for a religion which unites them, Monsieur ; and when you have found it, come and tell me of it !

CLAUDE. Only by grace can the body and soul of man become a unity. Pray, and you shall find grace ! Here and now, a new world of life, of spirit, is waiting to reveal itself. The dayspring of its life shines upon the closed windows of your soul. Open ! and let it enter ! One single act, the motion of a moment, is sufficient, and the miracle will be wrought. You have but to repent, and you will be saved ; and your sins will be forgiven.

NINON. Yes, Monsieur, I believe you, I have but to repent. But I find that — so unnecessary, so impossible ! You speak of grace ; but he who offers grace should have it for demonstration. It was not by grace, but by subterfuge, that you gained admission. You had been told, it seems, that here philosophers were always welcome. I allowed you to come ; and I find that you are only a theologian.

CLAUDE. One who seeks only to declare the truth, Madame. How do you distinguish ?

NINON. Your philosopher, Monsieur — claiming no plenary inspiration — admits in the first place his lack of knowledge ; from that he starts, seeks, adventures, and discovers at the end that he still knows very little. Your theologian, on the contrary, claims knowledge all made to measure beforehand ; so proceeds to impose it.

CLAUDE. The Truth, Madame, was before all things. And he to whom by grace it has been revealed, must seek of necessity to confer it on others.

NINON. Imposing as findings what may only be his own leavings, Monsieur. . . . That offends you ? Your theologian will not have his fabulous foundations disputed. No : he does not argue, or merely differ ; he is shocked, scandalised. And, if you continue to argue with me, I fear I shall not avoid shocking you. For you are no saint, Monsieur. Indeed, since I am as doubtful of your virtue as you are of mine, how is all this likely to end ?

CLAUDE. I am prepared, Madame ; I am armed ; I am not afraid of you.

NINON. I did not mean that I should try to seduce you, Monsieur. You do not sufficiently appeal to me.

CLAUDE. It is good of Madame to give me that reassurance.

NINON. I hope you did not need it. But though you and I have no temptation for each other in the accepted sense, nevertheless you have come to tempt me — as you yourself have admitted — in a direction where I fear I should lose myself. And I still fail to see how you would make grace, with all its accompaniments — repentance, penance, pardon for a past which in retrospect still delights me — how you would make that attractive to me.

CLAUDE. I myself may fail, Madame ; yet I hold this hope (it would be a sin against charity not to do so) that in the end, if you live long enough, your eyes will be opened, and you will see differently.

NINON. Yes, Monsieur, in age one must expect to see differently ; but it is not the time for good eyesight. I daresay you are right ; I can foresee something of the kind myself. For when I have lost all the pleasures of life — health, charm, appearance, sight, hearing, society, lovers, appetite : then I shall have to find — other interests. And since the Church is there ready (but not *your* Church, Monsieur) — courteous, confident in its waiting — perhaps : who knows ? I might do worse ; but I should do better, I think, to die sooner.

CLAUDE. Alas, Madame, alas ! If men's blind prayers and wishes were all answered, could Hell contain the number that would be found there, desirous to enter ? You ask me how repentance and penance can be made attractive. I answer — only by trial. For that spiritual adventure you must risk your " philosophy," Madame. It is necessary for the soul to have experience of them : then it will find itself.

NINON. Well, Monsieur, I have experienced repentance and penance ; but they have not attracted me.

CLAUDE. You did then once, if but for a moment, admit to yourself that you had done wrong ? You saw the error of your ways ; and wished that you had done otherwise !

NINON. Several times, Monsieur. But what of it ? We all make mistakes — before we have had experience. My first caprice proved to be a mistake ; but as I learned from it, those that followed mattered less.

CLAUDE. Caprice ? What do you mean by " caprice," Madame ?

NINON. I mean love, Monsieur. Love being so capricious, that is the best word for it. It also helps one to a recovery. . . . It did not take more than a day — and a night — when I first followed my inclinations " capriciously," to find that I and their object did not suit each other. As I was then only fourteen, I trust that even Monsieur will find it in his heart to pardon me.

CLAUDE. Oh, miserable, miserable world ! What filth and corruption one finds in you !

NINON. He was as rude, in his approaches — to the subject — as you, Monsieur.

CLAUDE. Continue, Madame ; though every word that you speak makes it harder for me to listen to you !

NINON. If you come to impart grace, Monsieur, a certain intimacy — a little undressing, shall we say ? — is necessary. Life, — the body, we are told, is more than raiment. And though in the life of such a one as myself the toilet has its place, it has also its displacements.

CLAUDE. You make it difficult for me to reply, Madame.

NINON. That is as it should be, Monsieur : morals are difficult things. For me they are also doubtful. How should I even begin to believe in them, when — as the first act in your temptation you drive me out of a garden into a wilderness ? No, Monsieur ; to make your temptation effective, you must drive me into the world, society, and show me there (where the Church maintains her position by bandying compliments with the Cæsars and the Cleopatras of rank, fashion and power) how much happier I should be if I acquired a reputation, like theirs, and lived a life — like theirs.

CLAUDE. In what respect " like theirs," Madame ?

NINON. In the respect the Church pays them,

Monsieur : the Reformed Church no less than the old. The Church consorts with Kings, Monsieur, in spite of what goes on behind the curtains. Is secrecy, concealment of the facts, her price for compromising with fornication and adultery ? If good behaviour in society is all she demands, why does she not consort with me also ? I, outside the curtains, am equally respectable in my behaviour. I not only observe the conventions, I impose them.

CLAUDE. On whom ?

NINON. On my lovers, Monsieur ; the congregation of faithful ones that I have always about me.

CLAUDE. Is it possible — that you allow them to *meet*, Madame ? Together !

NINON. I have made it possible, Monsieur. That, indeed, is my method : it is an education for them, a test of character. By their ability to meet each other — *with grace*, Monsieur — I judge whether they are worthy of — Heaven.

CLAUDE. It pleases Madame to jest——

NINON. It does, Monsieur.

CLAUDE. Of holy things, I was about to say.

NINON. Oh, no ! I was talking only of myself.

"Heaven" is an expression used by lovers—you may have forgotten it—of that favour which they so greatly desire : more often, perhaps, before than after it. When they continue, after the favour has been conferred, to call it Heaven— then, surely, they may in a sense claim to have attained Heaven : by whose grace, it is not for me to say, Monsieur.

CLAUDE. But is that a Heaven which you believe will last, either for you or for them, in the next world, after death ?

NINON. If life goes with us when we die, Monsieur, must not Heaven go with us also ? I have not been able to separate life—in its more fortunate moments—from what is called Heaven ; and I cannot imagine a better, except as I can imagine a more perfect lover than I am ever here likely to encounter.

CLAUDE. That Lover exists for every poor sinner. You have but to turn and look ! He is already there waiting to receive you.

NINON. The eternal love ! A parable, Monsieur, full of beauty. In her recognition of human need, the Church has always known how to turn it to her own advantage,—deceptively, it is true. If you could win me at all, Monsieur, it would be with the promise of such a lover. But in the religion of society, he does not exist : and the Church has no estate so honourable to offer me, in the matter of lovers, as that which I have made for myself. You looked surprised, Monsieur ; but now I am going to permit myself to speak freely and without mockery : and you who came to reproach me in the name of morality must listen while I tell you how that morality appears to me, how it disgusts and revolts me, making hateful to me the very name of religion, so long as the two stand allied as now. Monsieur, I have been free (as no wife can be free) to give my love when I wish to give love : then and then only. If you talk of morality, that seems to me, for a woman, not merely the most important morality—but all morality in a nutshell ; the first and greatest commandment. I leave to the Church to satisfy its own conscience over the moral imposition which it lays on all women whose nuptials it consents to bless. " You must not," it says to them, " refuse the demands of your husbands, however extravagant, lest by depriving them of their ' rights,' you induce them to fornication." In refusing the similar demands of my lovers, I have had no such moral dilemma set before me—the call to sin against nature, in myself, or them. Rather for me has it been the case that, while controlling them to virtue, I also reverted, momentarily, to chastity.

You make religion important; but here for me is the supreme test of it — that it has made nature a sin, and unnaturalness a virtue. And while it exalts " chastity " as a holy state, it turns upon the unfortunate victim whose nuptials it celebrates and forbids her to be chaste, of her own motion, even for a day, lest she drive her owner into sin.

Opposed to all such morality, I have made a society of my own. Compare my court, Monsieur, with that of Versailles. You will find it the more intelligent, the more cultured, the more natural, yet the better in its manners and deportment — in a word, the more decent. I do not permit rivalry; it may exist, but it must not display itself. Those who could not be courteous together had to go. It was a test: I sent many away. Those that remained I trained in virtue.

CLAUDE. In what virtue, Madame?

NINON. Hope. They learned — to hope without making any disturbance about it; and found it — trying perhaps, but delightful. I cannot doubt that it was good for them. Indeed, Monsieur, I think it was from me that some of the first gentlemen in France got their only lesson of self-discipline — in that one matter at least of which I have professional experience. Many I must have made better husbands because I did not always extend to them the final favour, at their own time, and upon their own terms. But did their wives thank me for it, or even know of the service I had rendered them ? That was not to be looked for.

CLAUDE. You are telling me all this as a justification for your mode of life, Madame ?

NINON. No, Monsieur, my own conscience is at rest ; and to you I have no particular wish to justify myself. Your condemnation leaves me indifferent. But if I can instil in you a little shame, or uneasiness, over that morality which you and your institutions defend, I shall have done you also some good — made you, too, a little more civilised — as I have others, whom I liked better. . . . Wait, Monsieur, till I have finished ! . . . In the world, as we women have it presented to us, I see a double process at work. Outwardly and materially, in all its forms, laws, ceremonies, customs, society is made by men ; but inwardly it is women who insensibly reshape, control, modify, what men impose. The Church, perceiving this, with the wisdom and subtlety of the serpent, has bound women in a deeper allegiance and service to herself than she has men. In the humbler position in which she has placed them, they are more devout, more numerous, and more assiduous in their ceremonial attendances, more solicitous in the pious upbringing of their children. Submission for them has become the fundamental virtue, and the Church depends on it. So, to the measure of her success, the world remains male in its arrangements ; for though Mother Church has wisely assumed our sex for the purpose of symbolising the faith, it is none the less emphatically a faith which men have in themselves as the superior instruments of Heaven. And so, Monsieur, while the Church is in the ascendant — with women so much more ardent and regular in their practice of the Sacraments than men, — you have the world, society, safely in your own keeping; and the root of this successful prescription I presume to be " the Eternal Lover," symbolised in the fact that all three persons of your Godhead — are male, Monsieur.

CLAUDE. If you have finished, Madame, I will go.

NINON. By all means, Monsieur. To your Church this message : If you wish to preserve morality in its present form, continue to preach the submission of women as a dogma of faith. For if that goes, the faith may go also !

CLAUDE. I understand, Madame, the uselessness of further words. There is an abasement of mind which lies beyond me. The mercy of God alone can fathom and bring light into such darkness. My task must be to pray for you. Only one thought I would now leave to your conscience : small and unimportant though it be, it may touch some chord of common charity in you, where the higher appeal has failed. I, a fellow-sinner, but one who has found grace, stand before you in peril of death. To that, only grace could have brought me. Coming here to speak to you as I have done — I, a Minister of the Reformed Church, have risked not only my liberty, but my life. In thus seeking the conversion of one outside my own communion I have incurred penalties which with the lifting of a hand you may invoke ; and your unsupported testimony would be sufficient against me — even were I to deny. Denounce me, Madame, if you will ; but whatever you do to wipe from your memory the message I have here delivered, I shall still seek to accomplish by prayer that for which argument has proved powerless. And so, Madame, with all respect, I leave you.

NINON. Is that true ? Then, Monsieur, I respect — not indeed your judgment or your behaviour, only your courage. As to that — be assured, I give you safe-conduct. With your life, though not with your morals, you can trust me. But you — do you truly respect me ? Am I, in any way that you can understand or name — a person to respect ?

CLAUDE. I respect, Madame, that in you which

is in all of us — a soul destined to eternal life or death, which some day God, not man, must judge.

NINON. And for which then, I hope, God — like you His Evangelist and Minister — will also have — respect. Respect! I shall say to Him, as I say to you, Monsieur; " I belong only to myself till one stronger than me masters me. If that is done with my full acceptance, it wins my approval, my respect, my allegiance. But if otherwise, then I have no respect for it whatever — only contempt, hatred, defiance!" I live in hope, Monsieur. You tell me that God is a great lover. Perhaps, some day I shall accept Him — as mine. That will be interesting!

CLAUDE. (*For whom words are now over, making a profound bow.*) Madame!

NINON. (*Rising, and descending in a deep curtsey.*) Monsieur.

> (*In another moment the door is between them ; a few moments later another door sounds, and the house is quit of him. Ninon rings a handbell. Timorous and conscience-stricken, Nannette appears ; she holds to the door-handle for support, till, greatly relieved, she discovers that her mistress is requiring her assistance.*)

NINON. Oh, Nannette, where are you? Oh,

open the window and bring me my salts ! How naughty of you, Nannette, to let that man in ! He has been trying to seduce me.

NANNETTE. (*Horrified.*) Oh! Madame! It is not possible !

NINON. It *was* not possible, Nannette. I have withstood him to the death. . . . Why did you let him in ?

NANNETTE. I thought him so good, Madame,— and that he intended — but only well.

> (*But the honest girl has recollections, which cause her to add :*)

And, after all, he was a man, Madame — like other men.

NINON. (*With charity of understanding.*) You are forgiven, Nannette. . . . Yes ? Well ? What?

> (*For Nannette, it seems, has yet something to say.*)

NANNETTE. Monsieur himself is waiting below, Madame. When he came, I told him Madame was engaged.

NINON. He has been waiting long ?

NANNETTE. Almost all the time, Madame.

NINON. But how amusing ! Go, Nannette ; tell Monsieur I am now disengaged.

(Left to herself she sits thinking, and smiles : looks attentively into her mirror, and touches here and there the imperceptible wrinkles which no one else can discern ; and so doing she breathes to herself a gentle word of admonishment :)

Now, Ninon, be wise ! Do not repent !

(She is continuing her study when the door opens to admit Monsieur de Sevigné, the younger, a very graceful figure of cultured youth, who, with an air of intimacy which puts manners into second place, makes no formal bow upon entry.)

NINON. *(Regarding him from her hand-mirror.)* Monsieur is late.

SEVIGNÉ. *(Stiffly.)* On the contrary, Monsieur has been waiting—a long time.

NINON. My Nannette failed to report Monsieur's arrival.

SEVIGNÉ. " Madame's Nannette " informed Monsieur that Madame had a prior engagement.

NINON. Very true ; but engagements can be broken—if one wishes.

SEVIGNÉ. This one, Madame appears to have found interesting. It lasted a long time.

NINON. Monsieur repeats himself.

SEVIGNÉ. Since Madame, it seems, was similarly occupied.

NINON. That is true, Monsieur ; for a moment ago I was making discoveries which I have made before — but have neglected.

SEVIGNÉ. If Madame will be so good as to explain ?

NINON. (*With a gesture towards her mirror.*) There, . . . and there . . . and there.

> (*She is irresistible apparently. As he approaches, the stiffness goes out of him.*)

SEVIGNÉ. What am I to see ?

NINON. The inevitable, Monsieur ; old age beginning to show itself. Is it of that you are jealous ?

SEVIGNÉ. (*Surrendering himself.*) You lie, Ninon! Beautiful wretch, you lie !

NINON. That is a very sweet and comforting accusation, Monsieur. Repeat it often, so long as you can do so — with conviction.

SEVIGNÉ. Cruel also ! Why do you so mock and hurt me ?

NINON. (*Kindly.*) Because, cher ami, without pain there could be no pleasure ; because a little jealousy is still so good for both of us — has been, I mean. But to-day there must be an end to it.

SEVIGNÉ. Impossible. Not till my love changes shall I ever cease to be jealous.

NINON. You are right, Monsieur. Practised in moderation it is one of the entertainments of love; without moderation it becomes a barbarism. But when old age withdraws one to a life of meditation — the occasions for jealousy are over.

SEVIGNÉ. (*Seizing her with ardour.*) Ah! Kiss me, Ninon! Kiss me!

NINON. (*With self-possession.*) Is Monsieur intending to take what is not offered?

SEVIGNÉ. (*Releasing her.*) Have I ever disobeyed your command, Ninon — your slightest wish?

NINON. Never; except when I wished you to, Monsieur. Now I bid you to listen. (*She arranges herself for the recital into an attitude of meditation.*) If I told you, dear friend, that I have received a call — a conversion — would you believe me?

SEVIGNÉ. A call? . . . To what?

NINON. It is a little gauche that you should make me find words for it. . . . To what the world calls " respectability," and the Church " chastity."

SEVIGNÉ. I should only believe that you were mocking — deceiving yourself — or allowing another to do so.

NINON. Ah, no! Do not suggest it! I am my

own convert. But that he should have happened to-day of all days is certainly very provoking !

SEVIGNÉ. Something has annoyed you ?

NINON. Why, yes ! For it is annoying to find that which one knows to be wise made to look foolish : a trial to one's pride — tempting one to *be* foolish in the opposite direction.

SEVIGNÉ. I agree : but I shall agree better when you have explained better.

NINON. Is it not annoying, mon ami — when one has decided for one's self by what road to reach the palace of wisdom — to meet an owl sitting on a scarecrow that points in the same direction, and have it hooted in one's ears ?

SEVIGNÉ. An owl ? Ah ! did I, then, an hour since see it at your door ? — a black owl with a white ruff to its neck, was it ? As I came it preceded me ; and it did occur to me then, to wonder (while I was so kept waiting) what a bird of that plumage could be doing in *your* nest.

NINON. I did my best to make *him* wonder also.

SEVIGNÉ. And now, filled with that wonder, he has dismissed himself ?

NINON. But has left me his scarecrow.

SEVIGNÉ. If it be only a scarecrow, *you* will not be scared by it.

NINON. It spoils the picture ; shadowing the road, there it stands — pointing.

SEVIGNÉ. A moral ?

NINON. Two : contradictory ones.

SEVIGNÉ. Come ! What is the heart of this mystery ? — may I not be permitted to know ?

NINON. The heart of it will disappoint you, my friend ; at least I would hope so : and yet must hope not, since I want you — even with a little regret — to agree.

SEVIGNÉ. With a little regret, I reply that you are speaking in riddles — but still charmingly. Cannot those lips, for a moment, express themselves more simply, more directly — more intimately ? May I not——?

NINON. No, dear Monsieur, be content ; kiss only my hand, and I will tell you. (*She pauses to permit the endearment, then resumes.*) Dear friend, I that am old enough to be your mother, have been foolish enough to be your mistress, for how long is it now, since we first met ? Years, months, minutes ?

SEVIGNÉ. I have never yet wanted either to count or to distinguish them. But since you ask, let us say the minutes have gone, and the years are to come.

211

NINON. No, my friend : undeceive yourself ! The years cannot ; we have had them. I *have* counted, on a dial that tells me the truth — only too well. The minutes have mounted to hours, the hours to months, the months to years ; and the years that strike — unlike the hours, cannot be repeated. Love does not live by decades in such frail vessels as we ; nor will all these kisses on my hand save it from the lines which are there already, waiting to become visible.

SEVIGNÉ. Ah, no ! To my eyes never ! They shall not !

NINON. Do eyes, then, really wish to be blind ? I heard that said to-day by the owl sitting on its scarecrow ; and denied it to be true. Now you convict me, that it can be. But don't let us argue, my friend ! Of that, for one day at any rate I have had enough. That scarecrow owl, how he has tired me !

SEVIGNÉ. By his argument, or only by his existence ?

NINON. Why, it is only by argument he exists ! As for his facts, I deny all of them ; they belong to a different world.

SEVIGNÉ. That does not disprove them.

NINON. No ; but it removes them — to where proof is not possible. He, it seems, is to have his world, and be as sure about it as he will ; I not to have mine, but be dragged into his dream, and there perish — cease to be the thing I am ! And I have only to look up at the stars to see how improbable — that this microscopic world of ours, single and self-contained, should be the ultimate reason for a whole universe and hold the secret of it ! Why, it is as reasonable as for a centipede to move upon only one leg !

SEVIGNÉ. So you, too, believe in " other worlds," Ninon ?

NINON. When I get to them. But while I am on this one, I will not have my feet argued from under me, and their right to dance denied me !

SEVIGNÉ. What was the argument ?

NINON. Perdition — for those who will not think as he does ! Mon Dieu ! What a God he has tried to set before me — monstrous, unbelievable !

SEVIGNÉ. Is any kind of a God — believable, Ninon ?

NINON. Believable ? How can one say one believes where one *knows* nothing, but only imagines, dreams, hopes ? And yet I believe in the stars, about which also I know nothing. What is belief ? Philosophy would have us doubt whether anything material exists at all. But if, as Monsieur Descartes assures us, existence is only thought—then, it is because God has thought about us that we exist ; and, since we have paid Him the return compliment, He also exists—by mutual arrangement. And, for this day at any rate, I have thought enough about morality for that also to exist,—a poor little bastard, begotten while its parents were having a bad dream !

SEVIGNÉ. The parents being——?

NINON. Enough to know, Monsieur, that the Church has adopted it, and that the World also pays to it a certain attention. Do not inquire further !

SEVIGNÉ. No, Ninon ; you are *not* tired ! You are adorable !

> (*And again he makes a tender advance which she restrains.*)

NINON. Monsieur has already sufficiently expressed himself.

SEVIGNÉ. But still I say " Ninon," and shall continue saying it.

NINON. Well, that is more true than saying " Madame "—a title which I affect with insufficient qualification. But let us not now talk of ourselves any more, but of better things—things which will last longer, and always be good for us to remember.

SEVIGNÉ. Let us talk of love, Ninon.

NINON. Of love ?—in general, you mean ? for, in the particular, the individual self is more lasting. Though there are privileged souls capable of finding in love a reason for continuing to love always.

SEVIGNÉ. Love meaning—what ?

NINON. An adventure, my friend, in which, if one stops to think, love is over.

SEVIGNÉ. In your own life, Ninon ?

NINON. Many times I have stopped to think, Monsieur ; and then, in place of adventure, has come—fear.

SEVIGNÉ. For what ?

NINON. For one's faith, Monsieur. It needs, for a woman, a hundred times more esprit, more confidence, more courage, to give oneself to love than to command armies. What is love but the defenceless surrender of one's whole life to invasion, and yet to remain conqueror ? For a woman what more perilous adventure can there be ? It is a religion, which may include martyrdom. And this love, this adventure, proves so often to be only a caprice—a piece of music which must by its very nature come to a close—finish. To many that have played accompaniment to my caprices I have indicated the closing passage—advising them that the caprice was over—the harmony ended. And as, for so many who have sought to prolong that which we played together, I have softly closed down the instrument while their hands still lingered upon the keys, reluctant to let go—so now to myself I must, in prudence, give the same advice when the reluctance is mine.

SEVIGNÉ. *Our* music is not yet over, Ninon !

NINON. Yours is not, my dear. Play it with others ! I am speaking only of myself. For me the days of the instrument are over. But there it will remain—capable de tout—cherishing in silence the ripeness of tone which years have given to it, the music gone like wine into the wood : the time come when only in silence can it find safety.

Learn this of me, my dear ! Be watchful of love, lest it become a ghost. Friendship is different, and is the longer to be trusted. Passion is an appetite of the body, for which the mind has a taste also. But appetite diminishes, while taste, which is more critical, remains ; and an over-indulged or forced appetite spoils the taste. Of this, love must always beware. And since I have, up till now, nothing but pleasant recollections of you—you also of me, I hope—do not let me have to remember that I ever saw your eyes resting on me with the beginning of distaste or indifference.

SEVIGNÉ. Ah ! no, Ninon, never, never ! Yet that, if I understand you rightly, is what you now feel toward *me*.

NINON. No, Monsieur; that is where I am so wise. I still like—you still attract me—not a little.

SEVIGNÉ. You love me still, Ninon?

NINON. I love you still, Monsieur. The caprice has not ended.

SEVIGNÉ. How often, without caprice, *have* you loved, Ninon?

NINON. Without caprice, as an aid, never. Why ask? For arriving at the right choice, experiment is necessary, but numbers are unimportant. In my religion, I have never lacked worshippers; but have had few disciples—and, of my own sex, not one. For those with whom the world has chosen to class me, were by no means my disciples. In the intervals of their life—business—amusement—call it what you will—penitence and denial took hold of them; and in the shades of Holy Church they would kneel to be washed of their flesh-colour, to a pale leprosy still far from that pure tint of the lily they affected; and so—issuing from those holy shades to the light of day—found it so unbecoming, 'tis no wonder they became flesh-colour again. But that did not make them my disciples. And as for my congregation of worshippers, if they found me at all different from the rest, it was but to wonder—not understanding why.

217

SEVIGNÉ. I, too, have wondered sometimes a little—why you chose to be gracious—to so many, Ninon.

NINON. Because, Monsieur, I had a mind of my own, which I followed. I saw men enjoy a thousand liberties which women must not taste, which I wished to taste : therefore I made myself a man, so far as that was possible—claimed a man's privileges, and became—as there was no other way for it—a law to myself, a law-giver to others. I have conquered a society, Monsieur, which marriage would not have given me ; indeed have had more than I could find room for. For here again it is not numbers but choice which matters. My lovers I choose for one reason—my friends for another : Racine, La Fontaine, Molière, St. Evremont, Boileau—for friends, what could one wish better ? Also (when I chose) those who ceased to be lovers remained friends. Aye, and more than that : as one of holy repute receives the respectful salutations of the worldly, I (with a reputation less holy) have won the respect of those who are not of my faith, nor practise it. Thus I have made—a little unfairly, perhaps—the best of two present worlds.

And so, after it all, I feel wise,—wiser than Solomon, for, without his disillusion, I have lived a complete life.

SEVIGNÉ. Solomon also built a temple, Ninon.

NINON. Solomon had sufficient money to keep up two establishments, Monsieur, and to make for himself two very different reputations. But whatever form life takes for its completion, implies limitation. Venus in an evening sky : could you wish for anything more complete ? But there is the evening sky as well, and beyond it the universe.

SEVIGNÉ. "Venus in an evening sky ! " How perfectly, how adorably, in that phrase, you present yourself once more, as I have always seen you.

NINON. (*Speaking softly.*) This time to wish you a very good night, Monsieur. Aye, now we come to it ! The evening star knows its time, and sets before daylight is over. A temple ? I have no use for it. Give me a garden where I may end my days. That shall content me.

SEVIGNÉ. What flowers, Ninon ?

NINON. Memories, Monsieur.

SEVIGNÉ. Of your own making : delightful company !

NINON. Yes ; so long as one can dismiss them. If one cannot do that, memories become ghosts, and haunt one.

SEVIGNÉ. To haunt *you*, for me would be almost happiness.

NINON. Not if you wished to see *me* happy also. Be a ghost and you shall hear me say " I hate you ! "

SEVIGNÉ. Why should you hate a ghost, Ninon ?

NINON. Because it is the embodiment of selfishness, not even contented to remain in a world of its own — death inflicting itself back on life. What is more horrible, more despicable ? I once had a religious friend, who — because of his religion — died to me, and thereafter tried to haunt me ! In all the lives I have lived he is my one regret.

SEVIGNÉ. You regret parting from him ?

NINON. Rather that we ever met ! For, in his religion, I discovered him to be of a possessive and ghostly selfishness. He was — in the great world — a man of some importance ; when we first met merely an Abbé, which, though it imposed discretion in our relations, presented no hindrance. Presently he received warning that he was to become a bishop — a step, it was whispered, to even higher expectations ; whereupon he had an access of circumspection, and became chaste. And all at once, in the cupboard, I saw the skeleton that was to haunt me, and heard the rattling of its bones. That is a memory of which I would gladly rid myself.

SEVIGNÉ. What happened, Ninon ?

NINON. Finding that he must either give up me or his ambition, he endeavoured to lead me to religion, and teach me penitence ; so that, in renouncing possession, he might at least have the satisfaction of knowing that there would be nobody else. Like that other owl, upon whose going you waited, he insisted on leaving his scarecrow behind him.

SEVIGNÉ. Where did he plant it, Ninon ?

NINON. Here in my memory, Monsieur ; so that whenever I come to a parting, I am faced by the fear of again meeting that ghost, or one like it ! It recalls the story of Ignatius Loyola and the young man, to whom he was spiritual director, who loved too well one that had entered into the bonds of matrimony. You know it ?

SEVIGNÉ. (*Mischievously.*) I never know any story as you would tell it, Ninon.

NINON. But this one I could never have invented ; it is too terrible. To Ignatius, his friend and director, this young man had confided that on certain nights, in the husband's absence, he went regularly where he should not. And after many exhortations to penitence, and many failures to amend, he ceased at last to trouble his spiritual father's ear with a tale which had become monotonous.

221

Now it so happened that his way to bliss lay over river, by a bridge ; and it was winter. One night, as he crossed, he heard a voice from the water calling him by name ; and looking down, saw the head of Ignatius sticking up like a fish, neck deep, teeth chattering, and the voice of imposed conscience cried, " My son, where are you going ? " Honestly he confessed the truth, but was not for turning back : he was promised, the lady was expecting him. Then said Ignatius, " I shall wait here till you return." From that fishy answer he fled in horror ; but it was useless, the fish had already swallowed him : consciousness of his beloved director, waiting neck-deep in icy water, robbed him of felicity. Torch extinguished, he returned, and gave himself up to a captivity from which he was never able after to escape.

There is an example of religion for you ! — unconscionable, possessive, tyrannous to attain its end. What have you to say ?

SEVIGNÉ. Only that apparently it was successful.

NINON. As a rape, Monsieur, is sometimes successful. But this violation — not of the body but of the soul — this trading upon the generous instincts of his friend — was, surely, a darker deed. For here was a secret told in confession ; and if what the Church claims for confession be true, it should never have gone further. But it did. Ignatius, the spiritual director, betrayed the secret to Ignatius, the busybody, the meddler; and devised the betrayal so subtly, with so poignant a persecution of his own flesh, that the baseness of the deed escaped the notice of its victim.

SEVIGNÉ. And did you, Ninon, in the instance you speak of, undergo a like experience?

NINON. Just once, Monsieur.

SEVIGNÉ. May I know in what form?

NINON. A parade of self-possession, Monsieur; accompanied by a discipline of religious exercises which he did not keep to himself.

SEVIGNÉ. (*Incredulously.*) He made you share them!

NINON. He was my guest, Monsieur: it was for the last time. And that being so, he conceived it to be his duty toward God to give me a demonstration of his ability to bear pain.

SEVIGNÉ. And what did you do, Ninon?

NINON. I did the only self-respecting thing possible under the circumstances: I went to sleep.

SEVIGNÉ. You mean you pretended to?

NINON. Yes, Monsieur; that was the humiliation: that I could not.

SEVIGNÉ. And for that he remains in your memory, when otherwise you might have forgotten him ? He may have guessed it.

NINON. I should not have forgotten him ; for till then his self-possession had always attracted me. Like you—yes, there was a likeness—he had perfect manners, even when things did not please him. And then, suddenly, at the test of separation —from him take warning !—these failed him. Till then I had never met with better behaviour, more delicacy, finer scruples. He was a religious man : I was aware of it ; but until promotion threatened, it was never allowed to intrude. He kept his Deity to himself—elsewhere, and under control. In our days of pleasant association I never once saw him upon his knees repentant—except to me. Of course there were absences ; no doubt it was sometimes officially necessary that, before resuming his priestly duties, he should make confession and endure abstinence. But he never told me of his repentances, nor asked me to share them. Had he done so, what a number of little deaths would have dotted the course of our assignations, encounters, idyllic meetings—milestones to mortality : life would have become a cemetery. I was grateful to him for sparing me that ; more I was complimented by this recognition that one art should leave room to another, each on its own premises.

SEVIGNÉ. Do you regard religion, then, as one of the arts?

NINON. It is certainly not a science, Monsieur; and if its aim be to beautify life — why surely! But how seldom the religious succeed in applying it. They forget that this world is not an oratory; and are slow to believe that, for the vast mass of humanity, religion is rather more impossible than poetry or painting.

SEVIGNÉ. I have heard it claimed, on the contrary, that man's need for it is universal.

NINON. The claim, then, is a very foolish one. We don't — any more than we all need a doctor.

SEVIGNÉ. We shall all need *him* some day, I fear!

NINON. But why? Death is quite easy without him. A doctor may, by luck or by skill, enable one to live longer; but he does not enable one to die. In that, at any rate, one can do without him.

SEVIGNÉ. But never does.

NINON. But I shall — so far as spiritual doctors are concerned: at least I hope so, if in my old age something strange and new does not take hold of me. I have not the disease of religion, Monsieur; so have no use for its practitioners. There is an over-insistence about them which has always annoyed me — as would the inventor of some nostrum (or cure, maybe) were he to insist that all —

the healthy and the sick alike—should have it compulsorily poured into them, and then all give it their testimonials, and behave as though it had done them good. That is a tyranny, Monsieur, which I resent. Such a thrusting of religion upon those who wish to be free of it, was always indecorous and is beginning to be ridiculous. Conquering nations—Christian and Mohammedan—have, to be sure, carried their religion with them, and imposed it upon the vanquished : but that was done as a political expedient, or a military necessity,—an item in the subjugation of race. We in France, who have our own civilisation, do not need to be subjugated.

SEVIGNÉ. And yet, behind all, there must be some final truth awaiting discovery. And if so, would you not wish to inform yourself of it, for it would then be important ?

NINON. No, Monsieur,—why any more than of astronomy, or mathematics ? If I have a friend who is a professor of Greek, must he talk Greek to me ? (Indeed, he had better not !)—Must I learn it ?—Or mathematics, because mathematics happen to be true ? Or know the distance of the earth from the sun ? These are things I can live without knowing. Life—the living of it—is the only valid proof of what is, or what is not, necessary—to salvation.

SEVIGNÉ. I am interested in your argument, since sometimes I have had the qualms of an inherited conscience. Not long ago a priest, to whom, in filial duty I submitted myself, not very willingly—a birthday present to my mother of her own choosing—he asked me whether I was truly intending to make my peace with God. I said : " No, only an armistice." It was an honest answer ; since surely I meant to return to you, Ninon : but from his point of view insufficient—to salvation. How do *you* interpret that word— salvation ?

NINON. By living, Monsieur. Sufficient unto the day is the salvation thereof. So long as I live, paying my debt to life, as it comes, bringing evil or bringing good—and finding the exchange worth it—I am saved for the day at any rate ; and can look forward with reasonable hope to more salvation on the morrow. We have the world as we find it ; and each applying our own solution of life, we extract from it our interests and our pleasures ; and we pay its taxes in pain, grief, occasionally in loss of fortune—finally of life itself. We meet it as it meets us. Am I to be told that behind these contacts of life (with which we are so intimately bound up) something has carefully concealed itself from our senses, claiming from behind that concealment conformity to a set of laws other than

227

nature's, and waiting to spring out on us with demonstrative and vengeful proof of its existence after we are dead ? Monsieur, if that is the God of religion — making such claims, under such conditions — I will meet Him to His face, if ever I have to meet Him — and say, " You are no gentleman ! " I was never yet capable of making a lover of one who was not a gentleman. And upon that will depend whether, in a future life, I can pay more attention to its pleadings than I have in this. But, religion is not so unteachable as it pretends ; and often the Church, in spite of her stage-thunders, has known how to be wise. Was it not a certain court Abbé who, when called upon to attend in spiritual disease and bodily decay a lady who for many years had found royal favour, and feared that Heaven might take an ill view of it, — was it not this Abbé who then had to reconcile his religious precepts with his more gentlemanly instincts ; and so, when his spiritual patient told him that she feared she was going to be damned (for to that depth of despondency had disease carried her) — found the good manners to reply : " Heaven will think twice, Madame, before damning a lady of your quality."

You laugh, Monsieur ; but believe me, breeding belongs to the soul enough to make the thought ridiculous that a person of fine breeding is fit only for damnation. Yes ; religion must learn to adapt itself to the scruples of humanity and good breeding, if it is not to lose standing, and become merely the device of fools and vulgarians, for exercising an influence which in other directions they lack.

The Church's adoption of a policy of persecution was more a betrayal of good manners than of good morals ; and this Protestantism which it has produced is exactly the punishment she deserves — that the religion of half Europe has now become something which one cannot possibly associate with a sense of high breeding.

SEVIGNÉ. I have never heard you speak of religion before, Ninon. I did not know that it interested you.

NINON. Religion does not interest me, Monsieur ; but its social and intellectual encroachments do of necessity ; since my own liberties and enjoyments are of an intellectual kind. And today I have had an annoying experience when circumstances made it least welcome. If professors of religion wish to visit me, they are welcome as other professors of the sciences and arts, not for their eminence in any special department of knowledge or piety, still less for any attempt to impose it, as the price of their acquaintance, upon others ; but merely for their social qualities. Let no doctor talk to me of his operations, nor any apostle or evangelist about the curing of souls, seeing that in all churches boxes are provided, where that can be done in private which in public ceases to be decent. And similarly, my dear, when that is over which has to be over, do not talk about it, as though it were your right to do so—to one who may be unwilling to hear.

SEVIGNÉ. Am I then to say nothing, Ninon? Do you forbid me to plead even?

NINON. Why go back, my dear, from a course that we have travelled so well? See how easily, in this last hour, we have changed from lovers to friends; and have still found much to say that was interesting. I owned that I was tired; and you, accepting my plea, have been contented. Before I tire, my dear, and before you tire—learn to be contented, like this, and like this.

(*With hands softly caressing his she continues :*)

In this hour that has grown dark without our perceiving it, we have made for ourselves an experience—a memory—that will last, and will always be pleasant to remember. And now I am going to tell Nannette to bring in the candles.

SEVIGNÉ. No, no! Not yet!

NINON. But I *want* my candles! For *this* Venus does not shine like that other without the aid of a

230

light for you to see her by. And I still wish that you should see me shine at my best before I go.

SEVIGNÉ. Go ? Where are you going, Ninon ?

NINON. To the country, and to friends — for rest, and change. When I return presently, come and see me again, if you like, — Monsieur.

> (*This time the word is said with a meaning :
> the lover perceives in it a change of
> relations.*)

SEVIGNÉ. You mean — " Monsieur " ?

NINON. Yes I mean " Monsieur." And I pay you a great compliment, Monsieur : the greatest that a woman of my experience can pay to anyone. Had you been my first lover — who knows ? But since that was impossible, I have made you my last.

> (*He bends down and lays his face upon her
> hand. She waits, then softly withdraws
> it.*)

And now that we have said " Good-bye," think of yourself a little, not of me. You are young, but have already come into your inheritance. You have a name, and an estate — honourable possessions — and for these you must do the thing which your birth requires of you. You know it well, Monsieur. The day of your marriage cannot be far distant ; and if this parting at all hastens it, I shall have done well by you ; also by her — who, if

231

you are wise, will never hear tell of me. From me she will receive, as her partner in life, one who has learned civility where it is most needed and least practised. I do not claim all the credit; the accomplishment was mutual.

SEVIGNÉ. You are very kind, Ninon; but your kindness only makes it more cruel! Yes, it is of your kindness now that I complain!

NINON. Keep your complaint, Monsieur! for while it lasts, it is a good one; and you will not die of it. . . .

(*So saying, she rings her hand-bell.*)

Lights, Nannette; bring in the lights!

(*And Nannette enters.*)

NANNETTE. Did I hear Madame ring?

NINON. For the lights, Nannette.

NANNETTE. I am bringing them, Madame. (*Going out for a moment, she returns with them.*) Does Madame know the time? Here is the carriage waiting.

NINON. Already?

NANNETTE. It has been here this half-hour, Madame.

NINON. Why, then, it is time, indeed, and we had forgotten it! Go, Nannette, fetch me my cloak, and wait for me. Good-bye, Monsieur.

No, do not go, stay ! It is my last command. I
have told Nannette that to-night you are my
guest. Here, in the house of the absent mistress,
sleep wherever you will. The memories are there,
and they are yours for the keeping. Think kindly
of me ! Complain, if you must, but sleep well !
oh, sleep well ! sleep well ! . . . Adieu, mon ami !
Au revoir, Monsieur !

> (*And with a sudden movement too quick for
> him to make any answer, she is through
> the door and is gone.*
>
> *He stands quite still, listening for a long time
> to the sounds of departure below. Pres-
> ently, behind him the folding doors
> softly open, showing a lighted bed-
> chamber, and a prepared meal. Nan-
> nette, who has made the preparation,
> comes out, and with an indicating ges-
> ture says :*)

NANNETTE. Voilà ! Monsieur est servi. Madame
wishes him a very good night.

> (*And Nannette, having thus fulfilled orders,
> goes leaving him alone to his reflections.*
>
> *He turns, goes into the inner chamber, and
> throws himself down upon the bed.
> " Ninon ! " he cries, but his heart is not
> going to break.*)

The Mortuary

Characters

JOHN DONNE.

NICHOLAS STONE.

THE HOUSEKEEPER.

JOHN DONNE
From an effigy by Nicholas Stone (St. Paul's Cathedral)

The Mortuary

February, 1631.

*Outside the Deanery of Old St. Paul's it is spring
weather ; but, except for a sense of brightness
coming through the windows, spring does not enter
here. The Dean has chosen a low vault-like
chamber in which to spread himself ; and on a
draped bench he lies hearsed, dressed as we still see
him in effigy, in a long knotted shroud, the head-
piece of which encloses the fine rather dry features
of a man who has lived well, in the world's accep-
tation of that phrase, and has come now to think
ill of it.*

*Over the sunk breast the hands are meekly folded ;
and with the face of an actor he simulates death ;
but at the opening of the door the eyes start into
life, and turn on the entrant a look of challenging
interrogation.*

*Nicholas Stone, carver and stone-mason, a man of
intelligent appearance, comes hastily forward,
bearing on a trencher a pile of modeller's clay,*

oozy with moisture. He wears the working smock of a plasterer, and his hands are whitened from labour upon the clay figure, which, lying alongside of its original in the flesh, now appears almost finished.

In some trepidation, under the flashing challenge of those dark eyes, the sculptor sets down his clay ; but before he can speak, the challenge has gone out of them, and a look of resignation takes its place.

STONE. I am very sorry, Mr. Dean, that I have kept you waiting.

DONNE. Do not be sorry, my friend ; I wait not for you, but for another. And when you shall have finished, that waiting will not be over.

STONE. You expect somebody, sir ?

DONNE. Aye ; if that which hath no body may be called " somebody."

STONE. (*Apologetically.*) Your pardon, sir, . . . I do not quite understand.

DONNE. Why, how should you, till I have explained myself ? Yet he that has explained himself has already passed from his first judgment, and stands prepared for his last.

STONE. (*Still at a loss.*) Sir ?

DONNE. (*Indulgently descending into plain speech.*) Come, come, Master Imager, try no longer to understand me ! Go on with your task !

I talk to you having none else to hear me, except it be my own conscience; and she an uneasy listener—I find you the more comforting.

STONE. Indeed, I am glad, sir, that I can be so; for to lie here so long and tiringly must be very discomforting. And in your own shroud, sir! Were I to do such a thing, 'twould fright me out of my senses.

DONNE. Or into them rather! Aye; when thus I first planned, it was to that end—to fright myself, and so to get the better of it. But now my fear is well over; Death hath so accustomed me.

STONE. Death?

DONNE. Is it not as a dead man that you see me lie here; and is not that your commission? Of what else, thus clad, can I be thinking?

STONE. Why, sir, surely of many things; so many, I cannot name them. You did not commission me, I think, to make this memorial of your person, but you thought also of the many that would come after to see it.

DONNE. Why, truly! And seeing, to be reminded how they also must die, and be clad like me.

STONE. For that, sir, a few words had sufficed. "Memento mori" were enough for them that can read Latin; and four words of English would do it also. But were I to give this a face unlike your own, would you, sir, be satisfied ? Nay, a skull in place of it would remind men as well or better of what must befall them. But you did not commission a skull, sir.

DONNE. I did not : yet would have done so, were this only for others to look on. But given I survive your handling, Mr. Imager, and this stretching on the rack of death that I here practise, then I plan to make this my bed-fellow — or so close that he shall seem like it — till comes my day to die.

STONE. Then, sir, you do make a most cruel use of me !

DONNE. Cruel ? To whom ? I but ask that you shape me as hereafter I shall be, when life is out of me, and death in.

STONE. And that is cruel of you, sir ; for no craftsman loves death, nor wishes to handle it. Nay, even when he makes for a memorial, 'tis as a reminder of life, doing in his own small way a work of resurrection — raising up that which is dust into a form that shall endure. But you, sir, ask to be reminded only of your atoms ? And I am to search not for the life but for the death in you ? Then I fear that for your satisfaction, Mr. Dean, or for mine own, my work must needs fail, since it cannot please both of us.

DONNE. I have no wish to be pleased by it.

STONE. That may be, sir ; as you would not be pleased to die, nor find dying pleasant. But for your own satisfaction you say you would have this speak of you as dead ; whereas, for mine—though I give to it the semblance of death—or of sleep, rather—I would have it tell of you as in life you once were.

DONNE. Aye ? Tell of what ?

STONE. The manner of man, sir, that you are.

DONNE. For that truly you must see deeply. Are you so much in God's counsels as all that ?

STONE. I would not so claim, sir. When I said " manner of man " I spoke rather of outwardness ; a man's " manner " being how he appears unto others.

DONNE. And from that same appearance what manner of man *do* you find in me ?

STONE. One so much my superior, sir, and also my better, that, by permission, I would so leave it.

DONNE. By permission you shall not ! In virtue of that superiority you suppose in me I command you to be open. Nay, do not hesitate, my friend : give me the whole truth of it !

STONE. The truth may be other than as I see it, sir.

DONNE. Very like ; yet if a man knew all that others lied concerning him, he would know himself better, and the more truly for it. Come ! treat me as I were a dead man, and you speaking to some friend. . . . This dead Dean, that was once poet, then preacher ; what of him ?

STONE. A great poet, sir, and a great preacher, I would say ; though neither poems nor sermons can I fully understand. For, I would say, sir, that you were a scholar before you were a Christian.

DONNE. Indeed, I was so formerly.

STONE. Even now, sir ; for to understand the whole of your discourse, a man must know at least three languages — Greek, Latin and Hebrew — besides his own.

DONNE. He needs not. I keep all my substance to the one language, and bring in the rest but to confirm, unto men of learning, the ground of my authority.

STONE. That may well be, sir ; but such a smiting of tongues constantly recurring doth confuse the ears and the understanding of common men such as I ; so that I say to myself often, " Had he not found God in all these languages, would he have such a faith as now ? " You seem, therefore, to me, sir, to have come to Christianity by scholarship, rather than to scholarship by Christianity.

DONNE. That is well said, and true. So far, then, you have convinced me. What comes next?

STONE. Why, sir, that you are a great preacher, no man, I think, would deny. But many, sir, do hold that your preaching is too great to be understood, even with the gift of tongues. And as I say, sir, often I understand not the words, yet do I seem to understand that which lies behind them; for oft times, when you have wept, I have wept with you. I have even, sir, seen the King weep; which no sooner he, than all the Court wept likewise.

DONNE. Aye; that have *I* seen also; and have then thought to myself, " What a waste of water is here, that shall wash nothing!" For think you any that so wept were the cleaner for it on the morrow, or remembered even what sense of words set them weeping? I also; for fine preaching that stirs up a concourse of people makes weeping to come easy. Tears are a trap which many preachers fall into; your man of eloquence shall find honest truth a hard matter to come by where a peroration of tears brings its own matter with it. But of this my profession enough said. What is your further reading of me?

STONE. Why, sir, judging by your face alone, and without having else read or heard, would not all agree that here is one shall be known for a gentleman of high mind, of dignity, of importance ; aye, and of pride also, as well-deserved and having a right to it.

DONNE. How has any man the right to be proud ? For surely when he comes to die his pride goes out and becomes nothing.

STONE. As I read this world, sir, there be many that *are* proud, and well approved for it, with less reason than yourself. And so, to my thinking, must it always be. If that, then, be human nature, who shall deny it ? Be as dead as you will, sir ; yet men, seeing this face, will say of you certain things that you were, and had a right to be. And here with my hands have I laboured to make that truth plain as I see it.

DONNE. But not as *I* see it. If I take not a hand in this, 'twill be as I suspicioned, and falsehood not truth will come of it. Mr. Imager, I will model this face for myself.

STONE. And pray, sir, how will you do that, not having the craftsmanship ?

DONNE. The craftsmanship is here ready-made, waiting in these lineaments, on which death shall lay his clay with no more need of a man's handling than had God at first to raise them out of it. Aye, let the clay come whereunto truly I belong, and that shall tell truth of me better than you and your skill shall do.

STONE. You mean, sir, that I am to make a mask of you ?

DONNE. I mean that you are to bring and lay on the materials ; and then it is I that shall make the mask, not you. And so giving up my face to burial ere it be dead, so from it on my death shall truth be told plainer than by word or epitaph : This is he which, preaching unto others, could not save himself from that kind which he was, and that unkind which henceforth he must remain : a shape of dust till the dust go out of it and bone only be left.

STONE. Oh, sir, talk no more on this fashion, or I shall dream of it !

DONNE. And why shouldst thou not dream ? Do not dreams for our better affliction come from God ?

STONE. Not all dreams, sir ; many have I, I know, which come from the Devil !

DONNE. Nay, if they put fear in you, is it not rather God showing you the Devil his like ? I once had a dream which put so much fear in me that I woke from it a changed man.

STONE. I have no doubt, Mr. Dean, that you could fright me in the mere telling of it. But would you not rather I went now to get my materials ?

DONNE. Presently, Master Imager ; but you shall hear my dream first ; for it was from that dream that I resolved on this which you are now doing for me. 'Twas through me that you came back into England, was it not ?

STONE. It was, sir.

DONNE. I promised you patrons and commissions ; and was presently told that you had done well. When we first met, in Paris, 'twas there and just then that I had my dream. And it was a haunted man that spake unto you ; and haunted still he speaks now.

STONE. (*Apprehensive and a little scared.*) Sir ! I would rather not !

DONNE. But I would rather, and will. Aye ! if I can put the horror into your heart, then from your heart it goes unto your hands, and this work will be as I wish it to be : Death, fearful, and horrible ; but for all the horror thereof, the fear of it over. That is *my* case, friend. I see death horrible, but no longer to fear it. Amen, so come quickly, Lord, Maker and Unmaker of men !

(*After the passion of that ejaculation, he pauses a moment, then resumes :*)

That night of my dream—away from my own

246

land—came true tidings for me : Death spake to
my reins ; and sleeping I awoke and saw my wife
that is now dead, but was then living, and near
of her time to be delivered—saw her plain, even
as now I see you, standing before me, bearing in
her hands a dead babe. Of her flesh and mine, and
of our joy in it, there was born Death—yea,
putrefaction of a life that had seen not light ; yet
unto it had God given a soul. And I,—taught by
that which was of her and me, and of our troth to
which, in my fashion, I had been faithful till then
—did in my whole being, as with the tasting of
lips, so partaking, and receiving to myself, did I
taste and know that corruption of the grave which
is the end of all earthly joy and felicity. And that
my babe, whose life had sprung from my loins,
with so much joy and so many embracements, and
with such binding together, that we twain
seemed verily to have reached Heaven and become entrants thereto—that same, even at its
coming forth, had changed into the very similitude
and substance of death. And all this I can tell ;
but not the shame, and despair, and horror of it,
which did then so enter into my soul that never
has it left me, day or night. Put that into your
clay for me, Master Imager, and you will have
done well !

STONE. Sir, I cannot : nay, and I would not !

DONNE. That have I perceived ; therefore (as I say) get me the material and I will do it myself.

STONE. It will need time and preparation, sir.

DONNE. Take it ! I will wait.

STONE. More than an hour, sir.

DONNE. What is an hour to one that awaits Death ?

STONE. Meantime, you should sit up, sir, and rest.

DONNE. I shall rest better, lying as I am. . . . Go ; wait no more on me !

STONE. But may I send no one else to be with you, sir : or to be in call ?

DONNE. I am better alone.

STONE. Very well, sir.

> (*And resignedly, but also with a little relief, he quits the uncanny presence ; and will not be in too much haste to return ; as why should he ? for the Dean knows well how to be good company to himself and to waste no time, seeing that those famous discourses, with which he moves multitudes, like charity, begin at home. Thus we have but to attend, and we shall hear one now.*)

DONNE. Aye ; " well " truly : if now truly

alone! But, O Maker God, what man was ever alone that hath all those his past lives to look into? Come ye, my seven past lives, that are mine enemies, how say ye? — will ye ever, for all my prayers and beseechings, leave me *alone*? Ye decked me in garlands that have become chains, so strong I cannot break them, so fast wound they cannot be put off. Listen, ye my seven lives, while I rehearse to you the desolation with which ye have compassed me about, as with seven deaths, the stench whereof hath gone not into the grave but into this being of my flesh that by no means may I put off till I be dead!

Every man born of woman hath his life between two graves, of which the womb is the first, the sepulchre coming after. And of these two is not the womb the more destructive, and the more terrible? For in the grave no harm can come by the body unto the life and soul that have passed from it : there corruption is harmless, giving sense and desire but to worms, which also in God's time shall die, and return unto their dust. But in the womb, the soul, not knowing it, lies already a prisoner ; yea, and hath reached her doom — God knowing it, not she. In the womb we have eyes and see not, ears and hear not — like those things of the deep-sea waters which come never to the light. There, in the womb, we are fitted for works of darkness, all the while deprived of any light whereinto we may escape : There in the womb are taught cruelty suckled on blood : there may have earned damnation though never to be born ! In the womb a child may become a murderer, yea, a parricide, that dying takes the mother's life with it ! O Death, how sharp there is thy sting ! O Grave, how great there is thy victory : not in man's end, but in his beginning ; not in the putting from him of the flesh, but in the taking on of his nativity.

Also in my mother's womb I lay in a winding-sheet — then, as now. But that I cast — not of mine own will : this of mine own will I put on ! Out of that other I came to prepare myself for this — from the greater to the lesser, from a winding heavier than lead into a folding of soft linen kind and gentle in its embrace : the last that I shall ever know !

How say we — God hath given this earth unto the sons of men ? Nay, how hath He given it ? For their bodies to be formed from it, and thereto at last to return and lie ? Here, then, I prepare myself for the only possession that shall always be mine. No land can I keep to myself, nor roof for dwelling ; but this only that is verily me, to the earth do I return. Seven bodies have I shed from me, one to each seven years of my sojourn upon earth : now am I come to my last body. All those have parted and dispersed, but this shall remain. Therefore is it the more consecrate and belonging to death ; and so belonging and remaining possessed, shall come also to resurrection again from the dead—for salvation or for damnation having no end. Thou body ! O thou body that shalt rise, how fearfully, and in what expectation of doubt must thou come to stand before thy Maker at the last !—flesh which now destined for corruption, shall then have become imperishable ; companion of my misery, then to become misery itself, or else be lifted up from past misery to bliss in worlds that have no end !

O God, who has smitten me in my pride, here is my pride all laid prostrate before Thee, supplicant, asking of Thee but this—that Thou bring it to nought ! Yet how shall that, which is so much myself, cease so that it be not ? For is not pride, which was the cause why Angels fell, more living and enduring than flesh ? Yea, how fast it clingeth to my soul, and darkeneth by its counsels when my body I have put off ! My passions I have put away from me, for not being in the likeness of Thy Passion ; my comforts I am willing to forgo ; yea, pains have embraced and found dear, as being an image of Thine own. But my pride how shall I put away, and make be as it was not ? For look—

when I humble myself, pride goeth with me;
when I deny and abnegate myself, it is with pride
that I do it. So much doth pride possess and con-
strain me, so much doth it comprise all that of
myself which I know, in being and belonging,
both substance and person; so much, when I say
"I" 'tis pride speaking; so much, when I look
into myself, it is pride there, as from a mirror,
reflecting me—how then, quit of pride, shall I
know at once so to remain myself, yet be of such
kind that I may come before Thee and there be
known? This, Lord, is the mystery of my being,
and the burden of sin laid on me ere I myself was
born. O Lord, I beseech Thee—since else I find
no way—take unto Thyself, and purge, and purify
—this pride which is *me*.

If pride could die, as surely love can die,
    I would stand pure
Before my Maker, when mine earthly last
Comes to draw out my past,
And lay it there, where all sin must endure
    For ever, or pass perished utterly!
O kill my pride! But let my love come back
With all its faults; so nothing shall I lack—
Though sinful be the showing—to make plain
How without love I lived in so much pain
That, like to Satan, I must nurse my pride
To mend the hurt of my sore-wounded side,

Whence love was rent away !
Lord, in that day,
Because love in me hath so often died
Of self-dealt wounds, pardon my deathless
pride,
And by my dying loves be satisfied !

(*He pauses exhausted ; then resumes :*)

To this, then, hath mortality brought me at the
last, O my seven lives !—how miserable, how
miserable a man were I—if I might not die !

Death ! Death ! Yea, come quickly, Lord
Death ! Save me, lest I perish !

(*And suddenly, thus crying out on death, he
falls into loud weeping : so loud that for
a long time he does not hear that knocking has begun at the door. Catching the
sound of it, he stops—his weeping
abruptly over—for it is the voice of his
housekeeper that he hears, begging ad-
mittance.*)

HOUSEKEEPER. Oh, Mr. Dean ! Mr. Dean !
What is the matter ? . . .

(*There is a pause : then again knocking ; and
the Dean, accepting the situation, returns reluctantly to life.*)

DONNE. Come in, woman !

(Fearfully she enters, a stout comely body with a sensible mind, but now somewhat panic-stricken.)

HOUSEKEEPER. Oh, Mr. Dean, sir, what are you doing to yourself?

DONNE. Letting myself be once more troubled by you, woman! What is it?

HOUSEKEEPER. *(Plunging honestly to the true purport of her errand.)* Shrove Tuesday, sir.

DONNE. And what of it?

HOUSEKEEPER. Why, sir, your dinner ready an hour ago, and all this time kept waiting. And it's pancakes to-day, sir, you'll remember.

DONNE. Pray, why should I remember pancakes? If *you* have remembered them, that is sufficient. Be satisfied if I eat them.

HOUSEKEEPER. *(With proper domestic pride.)* Which you always do, sir.

DONNE. And will again, though this be the last time.

HOUSEKEEPER. 'Tis always the last time with you, sir. If words could dig a man's grave, you'd have been in it five years ago. Oh, sir, how you do keep on it to tease a body! But there!

DONNE. If I tease any body, it is my own body that I tease—even as you tease wool and then wind, till it become a thread. Look on me, woman, and look on this ! What think you of it ? Will it be like me when I am dead ?

(*He points to the effigy, which she regards with respectful distaste.*)

HOUSEKEEPER. That, sir,—*that !* On my word, sir, I wouldn't like to say in your Reverence's hearing what *I* think of it !

DONNE. But in my Reverence's hearing, you *shall* say it. Speak ! and speak truth !

HOUSEKEEPER. Why, then, sir, if you'll pardon me, sir, it looks not like you at all, sir,—else I wouldn't be saying it. It looks like a man that, for things he's done, and for reasons you couldn't say, has gone into the pillory to please himself, and be proud of it !

(*This appalling revelation of himself is too much for the recumbent Dean ; and as the upper half of him spasmodically rises from the dead, the shroud at the thrust of the thin, bony arms, falls open, revealing the skeleton body, bare but for the death-sheet in which it has been wound. Shocked and terrified by this exposure of the flesh, the Dean's house-keeper flies to the door, and is already half-way through it before the Dean's*)

255

characteristically bilingual expletive has found utterance.)

DONNE. Retro me, Sathanas ! Woman, get out !

(He falls back panting, exhausted. But it is not the exertion that has prostrated him so much as the devastating discovery that, in spite of all his efforts to get away from himself, the life of the body stills chains him, and the manner of man he is is the manner of man he will always appear to future generations in that graven image of himself which he has been at such pains to set up. It does, however, suddenly occur to him that it will appear more ghostly and disembodied if, instead of lying down, he causes it to be stood upright. And so, upright it stands to this day — the gauntest thing in effigies that one could wish not to meet.)

Printed by
The Garden City Press Limited
Letchworth, Herts